Persepolis

T0248396

33 1/3 Global

33 1/3 Global, a series related to but independent from **33 1/3**, takes the format of the original series of short, music-based books and brings the focus to music throughout the world. With initial volumes focusing on Japanese and Brazilian music, the series will also include volumes on the popular music of Australia/Oceania, Europe, Africa, the Middle East, and more.

33 1/3 Japan

Series Editor: Noriko Manabe

Spanning a range of artists and genres—from the 1970s rock of Happy End to technopop band Yellow Magic Orchestra, the Shibuya-kei of Cornelius, classic anime series *Cowboy Bebop*, J-Pop/EDM hybrid Perfume, and vocaloid star Hatsune Miku—33 1/3 Japan is a series devoted to in-depth examination of Japanese popular music of the twentieth and twenty-first centuries.

Published Titles:

Supercell's *Supercell* by Keisuke Yamada

Yoko Kanno's *Cowboy Bebop Soundtrack* by Rose Bridges

Perfume's *Game* by Patrick St. Michel

Cornelius's *Fantasma* by Martin Roberts

Joe Hisaishi's *My Neighbor Totoro: Soundtrack* by Kunio Hara

Shonen Knife's *Happy Hour* by Brooke McCorkle

Nenes' *Koza Dabasa* by Henry Johnson

Yuming's *The 14th Moon* by Lasse Lehtonen

Forthcoming Titles:

Yellow Magic Orchestra's *Yellow Magic Orchestra* by Toshiyuki Ohwada

Kohaku utagassen: The Red and White Song Contest by Shelley Brunt

33 1/3 Brazil

Series Editor: Jason Stanyek

Covering the genres of samba, tropicália, rock, hip hop, forró, bossa nova, heavy metal and funk, among others, 33 1/3 Brazil is a series devoted to in-depth examination of the most important Brazilian albums of the twentieth and twenty-first centuries.

Published Titles:
Caetano Veloso's *A Foreign Sound* by Barbara Browning
Tim Maia's *Tim Maia Racional Vols. 1 &2* by Allen Thayer
João Gilberto and Stan Getz's *Getz/Gilberto* by Brian McCann
Gilberto Gil's *Refazenda* by Marc A. Hertzman
Dona Ivone Lara's *Sorriso Negro* by Mila Burns
Milton Nascimento and Lô Borges's *The Corner Club* by Jonathon Grasse
Racionais MCs' *Sobrevivendo no Inferno* by Derek Pardue
Naná Vasconcelos's *Saudades* by Daniel B. Sharp
Chico Buarque's First *Chico Buarque* by Charles A. Perrone

Forthcoming titles:
Jorge Ben Jor's *África Brasil* by Frederick J. Moehn

33 1/3 Europe

Series Editor: Fabian Holt
Spanning a range of artists and genres, 33 1/3 Europe offers engaging accounts of popular and culturally significant albums of Continental Europe and the North Atlantic from the twentieth and twenty-first centuries.

Published Titles:
Darkthrone's *A Blaze in the Northern Sky* by Ross Hagen
Ivo Papazov's *Balkanology* by Carol Silverman
Heiner Müller and Heiner Goebbels's *Wolokolamsker Chaussee* by
    Philip V. Bohlman
Modeselektor's *Happy Birthday!* by Sean Nye
Mercyful Fate's *Don't Break the Oath* by Henrik Marstal
Bea Playa's *I'll Be Your Plaything* by Anna Szemere and András Rónai
Various Artists' *DJs do Guetto* by Richard Elliott
Czesław Niemen's *Niemen Enigmatic* by Ewa Mazierska and Mariusz
    Gradowski
Massada's *Astaganaga* by Lutgard Mutsaers

Los Rodriguez's *Sin Documentos* by Fernán del Val and Héctor Fouce
Édith Piaf's *Récital 1961* by David Looseley
Nuovo Canzoniere Italiano's *Bella Ciao* by Jacopo Tomatis
Iánnis Xenakis's *Persepolis* by Aram Yardumian

Forthcoming Titles:
Amália Rodrigues's *Amália at the Olympia* by Lilla Ellen Gray
Ardit Gjebrea's *Projekt Jon* by Nicholas Tochka
Vopli Vidopliassova's *Tantsi* by Maria Sonevytsky

33 1/3 Oceania

Series Editors: Jon Stratton (senior editor) and Jon Dale (specializing in books on albums from Aotearoa/New Zealand)

Spanning a range of artists and genres from Australian Indigenous artists to Maori and Pasifika artists, from Aotearoa/New Zealand noise music to Australian rock, and including music from Papua and other Pacific islands, 33 1/3 Oceania offers exciting accounts of albums that illustrate the wide range of music made in the Oceania region.

Published Titles:
John Farnham's *Whispering Jack* by Graeme Turner
The Church's *Starfish* by Chris Gibson
Regurgitator's *Unit* by Lachlan Goold and Lauren Istvandity

Forthcoming Titles:
Ed Kuepper's *Honey Steel's Gold* by John Encarnacao
Kylie Minogue's *Kylie* by Adrian Renzo and Liz Giuffre
Alastair Riddell's *Space Waltz* by Ian Chapman
The Dead C's *Clyma est mort* by Darren Jorgensen
Chain's *Toward the Blues* by Peter Beilharz
Bic Runga's *The Drive* by Henry Johnson
The Front Lawn's *Songs from the Front Lawn* by Matthew Bannister
Hilltop Hoods' *The Calling* by Dianne Rodger
Hunters & Collectors's *Human Frailty* by Jon Stratton
Screamfeeder's *Kitten Licks* by Ben Green and Ian Rogers
Luke Rowell's *Buy Now* Michael Brown

Persepolis

Aram Yardumian

Series Editor: Fabian Holt

BLOOMSBURY ACADEMIC

NEW YORK • LONDON • OXFORD • NEW DELHI • SYDNEY

BLOOMSBURY ACADEMIC
Bloomsbury Publishing Inc
1385 Broadway, New York, NY 10018, USA
50 Bedford Square, London, WC1B 3DP, UK
29 Earlsfort Terrace, Dublin 2, Ireland

BLOOMSBURY, BLOOMSBURY ACADEMIC and
the Diana logo are trademarks of Bloomsbury Publishing Plc

First published in the United States of America 2023
Reprinted 2023

Cover design: Louise Dugdale
Cover image @ 333sound.com

Library of Congress Cataloging-in-Publication Data
Names: Yardumian, Aram, author.
Title: Persepolis / Aram Yardumian.
Description: [1.] | New York : Bloomsbury Academic, 2023. |
Series: 33 1/3 Europe | Includes bibliographical references and index. |
Summary: "Tells the story of an album of European electronic tape music that
emerged from the sounds of the Greek anti-Fascist resistance, bore witness to
the Iranian Revolution, and served as a precursor the
Industrial and noise scenes"– Provided by publisher.
Identifiers: LCCN 2022028587 (print) | LCCN 2022028588 (ebook) |
ISBN 9781501381515 (hardback) | ISBN 9781501381508 (paperback) |
ISBN 9781501381522 (epub) | ISBN 9781501381539 (pdf) |
ISBN 9781501381546 (ebook other)
Subjects: LCSH: Xenakis, Iannis, 1922-2001. Persépolis. | Electronic
music–20th century–History and criticism. | Music–Political
aspects–Iran–History–20th century.
Classification: LCC ML410.X45 Y37 2023 (print) |
LCC ML410.X45 (ebook) | DDC 786.7/5–dc23/eng/20220629
LC record available at https://lccn.loc.gov/2022028587
LC ebook record available at https://lccn.loc.gov/2022028588

ISBN: HB: 978-1-5013-8151-5
          PB: 978-1-5013-8150-8
          ePDF: 978-1-5013-8153-9
          eBook: 978-1-5013-8152-2

Series: 33 1/3 Europe

Typeset by Integra Software Services Pvt. Ltd.
Printed and bound in Great Britain

To find out more about our authors and books visit
www.bloomsbury.com and sign up for our newsletters.

Contents

Acknowledgments viii
Dramatis Personae ix
Preface xii

Introduction: 'Signal' 1

1   **The Voice of the Resistance** 13

2   **Paris, 1947** 23

3   **The Voice of the Avant-garde** 31

4   **The Voice of Cyrus** 45

5   **Shiraz, 1968–9** 55

6   **Paris, 1971** 65

7   **Persepolis, 1971** 75

8   **The Voice of Khomeini** 87

9   **Afterlife** 99

Notes 108
Photographic Credits 137
Index 138

Acknowledgments

While writing this book I came into contact with three scholarly communities, one devoted to Xenakis, another in some capacity to Iran, and the third to electroacoustic music. Several people have been very generous with their time and expertise, among them Sharon Kanach, Robert Steele, Daniel Teige, Mehdi Taheri, Nikos Ioakeim, Houshang Chehabi, Mâkhi Xenakis, Pierre Carré, Etienne Assous, Nancy Cantwell, Rachel and Alan Longstaff, James Harley, Giancarlo Toniutti, Naut Humon, Bob Gluck, Loris Tjeknavorian, Reinhold Friedl, Thomas Herbst, Joshua Charney, Heather Hughes, Mahyar Entezari, Shiela Winchester, Michel Shamoon-pour, Cyrus Kadivar, Asif Agha, Donna Stein Korn, Nouritza Matossian, Aria Minu-Sepehr, and Vali Mahlouji, as well as an anonymous reviewer.

Also, endless thanks to the Interlibrary Loan staff at the University of Pennsylvania's Van Pelt Library.

Dramatis Personae

Iannis Xenakis (1922–2001): Greek-French architect and composer of orchestral and electronic works, including *Persepolis*, which is the subject of this book.

Le Corbusier (1887–1965): Swiss-French architect and urban planner, regarded to be one of the fathers of modern architecture—employer of Iannis Xenakis from 1947–59.

Edgard Varèse (1883–1965): Innovative French composer who referred to his work as 'organized sound'; served as an influence on countless twentieth-century composers, including Xenakis.

Olivier Messiaen (1908–92): French composer and organist known for, among other things, his incorporation of birdsong transcriptions into his compositions—an early mentor to and supporter of Xenakis.

Pierre Schaeffer (1910–95): French broadcaster and acoustician, developer of the *musique concrète* technique, and founder of the Groupe de Recherche de Musique Concrète (GRM), a group of composers dedicated to the practice. Xenakis, while not a formal member of the group, developed some of his ideas and recorded at Schaeffer's studio in Paris.

Pierre Henry (1927–2017): French *musique concrète* composer and member of the GRM, as well as a pupil of Messiaen and an associate of Xenakis.

Reza Shah (1878–1944): Father of Mohammad Reza Pahlavi, instituter of socioeconomic reforms for which he is regarded as the founder of modern Iran.

Mohammad Reza Shah Pahlavi (1919–80): Also known as Mohammad Reza Shah, the last shah (king) of Imperial Iran prior to the Iranian Revolution of 1979; and economic modernizer who oversaw the organization of the 2,500th Anniversary Celebration of the Persian Empire.

Farah Pahlavi (1938–): Shahbanu (Empress) of Iran, wife of Mohammad Reza Pahlavi, and organizer of the Shiraz Arts Festivals, at which several of Xenakis's compositions, including *Persepolis* (1971), were played.

Reza Ghotbi (1940–): Director of National Iranian Television (NITV) (1967–79) and advisor for the Shiraz Arts Festivals, and cousin of Farah Pahlavi.

Ruhollah Khomeini (1900–89): Shia cleric, spiritual leader of the Iranian Revolution (1979), and founder of the subsequent Islamic Republic of Iran.

When they poured across the border
I was cautioned to surrender
This I could not do
I took my gun and vanished.
– Leonard Cohen[1]

The power of appreciating poetry is rare, generally speaking,
in France; *esprit* soon dries up the source of the sacred tears
of ecstasy; nobody cares to be at the trouble of deciphering
the sublime, of plumbing the depths to discover the infinite.
– Balzac

Peter Jennings: Ayatollah, would you be so kind as to tell us
how you feel about being back in Iran?

Ayatollah Khomenei: *Hichi* [Nothing].

Sadegh Ghotbzadeh (translator), incredulously: *Hichi*?

Ayatollah Khomenei: *Hich ehsasi nadaram*
[I don't feel a thing].[2]

Preface

It is rare that a record album should find itself wrapped up in an event as historically momentous as the Iranian Revolution. *Persepolis*, Iannis Xenakis's electroacoustic paean to Persian history, was premiered at the Fifth Annual Shiraz Festival on August 26, 1971, during the yearlong celebration of the 2,500th anniversary of the Persian Empire. Xenakis's work was poorly or ambivalently received in the Iranian press and by local students, who misconstrued its purpose and characterized *Persepolis* as an 'insult to Iran.' Thereafter, it became a footnote in the sad tale of Mohammad Reza Shah Pahlavi and the rise of clerical anti-modernity courtesy of the Ayatollah Khomeini. While the story of the Revolution can be told without mention of *Persepolis*, it cannot be told without an appreciation for the part the Shiraz Arts Festivals played in forming public sentiment in Iran at the time.

In 1979, in the aftermath of Revolution, Henry Kissinger stated at a dinner hosted by the Harvard Business School that he thought it was wrong for the United States to treat the Shah, a longtime friend of America, like a 'Flying Dutchman'[3]—a mythical ghostship condemned to wander endlessly, never permitted to make port. Kissinger's comments came as the Shah, chased out of Iran, wandered the world, looking for a place to live, and eventually die.

Although it might be too much to compare Xenakis to the Flying Dutchman, he did spend much of his life in exile from his homeland. Having fled Greece, due to his involvement in antifascist activities, he settled in Paris almost by accident and spent much of the rest of his life in France. Unlike the Shah, who never again saw Iran, Xenakis was permitted to return to Greece in later life. His work continues to enjoy devotion there, as evidenced by the centenary celebrations taking place in Athens this year, and he also spoke of a 'Greek responsibility' in certain of his works.[4] At the same time, Xenakis described himself as 'a wandering man, an "alien citizen" of every country (in art as well).'[5] (Even the root word of Xenakis's surname, 'xenos,' means 'foreigner.') The condition of exile should be borne in mind while listening to *Persepolis* and other of his works, for exile has a way of directing one's gaze both into the past and far into the future.

Introduction: 'Signal'

'What's this noise?' 'It sounds like a boiler room.' 'A rusty train in slow motion.' These were some of the responses I received when I played Iannis Xenakis's electroacoustic work *Persepolis* for friends and acquaintances while writing this book. 'Why a whole book about something that's just noise?'

Why, indeed.

On February 21, 1913 a crowd assembled at the Teatro Costanzi in Rome to hear works by composer Francesco Balilla Pratella. Most of them were season ticket holders, people who were expecting something fun and easy to digest, like, say, Puccini. But Pratella was part of a group of Futurist composers who were aggressively introducing new sounds and forms into classical music. To them, Puccini might as well have been the Monkees. The premiere of Pratella's *Musica Futurista per orchestra* went surprisingly well and the audience applauded. There were a few loud discussions by audience members, but they otherwise left the hall without incident. But on the second night, March 9, things went very differently. Shortly after the opening notes of *Musica Futurista* there was, as Pratella recalls,

> an infernal clamor, made up of whistles, applause, cries, acclamations, and invectives. The public seemed driven insane, and the frantic mass boiled and from time to time exploded in rage resembling a mass of burning lava during a volcanic eruption. Some threw upon the orchestra and also on me, the conductor, an uninterrupted shower of garbage, of fruit, chestnut cakes; others shouted themselves hoarse crying every kind of thing; some protested not being able to

hear; some became exalted, others infuriated, some laughed
and enjoyed themselves, others quarreled and started rows,
with frequent blows between friends and enemies.[1]

Musica Futurista, today, sounds uninspired and bland, almost
as if it had emerged from the very conservatories Pratella
loathed. Even with the ears of 1913 it is difficult to hear what
caused a riot. Along with the score of *Musica Futurista*,[2] Pratella
published three short manifestos. In these he leveled criticisms
at the Italian conservatories and their faculty for discouraging
innovation and experimentation. He encouraged students
to desert traditional music education and instead compose
from their own sensibilities, drawing their inspiration from the
modern world rather than copying the masters.

Only three months later, on May 29, in Paris, a similar
incident occurred at the premiere of Igor Stravinsky's *Le Sacre
du Printemps*. Performing that night at the Théâtre des Champs-
Elysées was the world-famous Ballets Russes under the direction
of Sergei Diaghilev, with choreography by Vaslav Nijinsky and
stage backdrops and costumes by the painter and theosophist
Nicholas Roerich. These combined elements promised Paris
theater audiences a memorable evening. The house was divided
between the upper crust and the artists of Paris, who had seen
Petrushka the year before and should have been well prepared for
the combination of folkloric paganism and Modernist bitonality.
What happened again that night was later called a riot, or near-
riot. Within the first two minutes of the opening melody and
before the raising of the curtain, boos, whistles, and catcalls rose
from the audience. Then, after the curtain rose and the dancing
began, the real chaos ensued. Audience members began
shouting indignantly and others shouted back in an attempt
to restore order. Reports of slapping, fistfights, foul language,
and even antisemitism—some of it perhaps apocryphal—are

contained in the over 100 newspaper and magazine articles devoted to the event.[3] The same articles, followed by more recent scholarship, have never been able to pin down exactly what triggered the audience's violent reaction: the ungraceful dancing, the bizarre costumes, or Stravinsky's dissonant music, which was described the day after the premiere by the well-known music critic Adolphe Boschot: 'But in the desire, it seems, to make something primitive, prehistoric, he [Stravinsky] has worked *to bring his music close to noise.*[4]

Ten years later, on March 4, 1923, at New York City's Klaw Theater, pandemonium erupted following the premiere of Edgard Varèse's *Hyperprism*, a piece that, like *Musica Futurista* and *Le Sacre du Printemps*, now hardly sounds radical. Nevertheless, the performance was interrupted throughout with laughter, catcalling, and hissing. The piece had to be repeated after certain elements had left the concert hall.[5]

There were in the same decade numerous such disapproving audience responses to Modernist classical music. Premieres of music by Alban Berg, Erik Satie, and George Antheil were also interrupted by outraged audiences.[6] In the 1960s, a Venice performance of *Intolleranza 1960* by Luigi Nono was interrupted by Fascist elements (who were evidently reacting to the political content of the opera more than the noise).[7] It is no coincidence that all the music subjected to this treatment was Modernist. It is also no coincidence that the audience responded to what they perceived as noise, with more noise.

Luigi Russolo, a Futurist theorist and composer, who was present at the riotous premiere of *Musica Futurista*, famously wrote of the event,

> On March 9, 1913, during our bloody victory over four thousand passé-ists in the Costanzi Theater of Rome, we

were fist-and-cane-fighting in defense of your Futurist Music, performed by a powerful orchestra, when suddenly my intuitive mind conceived a new art that only your genius can create: the Art of Noises, logical consequence of your marvelous innovations. In antiquity, life was nothing but silence. Noise was really not born before the 19th century, with the advent of machinery. Today noise reigns supreme over human sensibility. For several centuries, life went on silently, or mutedly. The loudest noises were neither intense, nor prolonged nor varied. In fact, nature is normally silent, except for storms, hurricanes, avalanches, cascades and some exceptional telluric movements. This is why man was thoroughly amazed by the first sounds he obtained out of a hole in reeds or a stretched string…. Nowadays musical art aims at the shrilliest, strangest and most dissonant amalgams of sound. Thus we are approaching noise-sound. This revolution of music is paralleled by the increasing proliferation of machinery sharing in human labor. In the pounding atmosphere of great cities as well as in the formerly silent countryside, machines create today such a large number of varied noises that pure sound, with its littleness and its monotony, now fails to arouse any emotion.[8]

Russolo is making the interesting argument that Modernist music (and perhaps visual arts, though he doesn't say so) was a response to Modernity itself. As factories, automobiles, railroads, and sirens proliferated, dissonance in music sharpened along with them. Music, he claimed on a more personal level, now had to compete with machines to 'arouse any emotion' in him. In 1913, Russolo and the Futurists were still promoting dissonant experimentation and the incorporation of non-musical 'noises' into orchestral music. He had no way of predicting what would happen four decades and two world wars later with the invention of the synthesizer and the electronic studio. He couldn't have foreseen Industrial Music (whose proponents, in the 1970s and 1980s, seldom if ever cited Russolo) or the phenomenon of 'noise music,' which has grown steadily since the advent of home taping. But he did foresee that noise would go places for a long time to come, and that the reactions to it would be violent.

When Russolo goes on to say that '[t]he ear of an eighteenth century man never could have withstood the discordant intensity of some of the chords produced by our orchestras,'[9] he is saying that a refinement, or at least tolerance to noise, is built along with life in industrialized societies. But he is also reminding Pratella, to whom his epistolary book is addressed, that all violent responses to Futurist and Modernist music are basically pro-conservatory or, as Russolo might have said, pro-mediocrity. From this perspective we can look at the near-riots in the concert halls, as reactionary—that is, a political reaction to a fear that harmony, and thus the very foundations of music itself, was being compromised. You can still feel the occasional aftershock today of this intellectual quake that erupted more than a century ago.

Dissonance was in the air in the 1910s, and so were new ideas about truth. Along with attacks on harmony in music and realism in painting, religious authority and Enlightenment science were weakening under the weight of ideas about randomness in nature (Darwin), the importance of perspective (Nietzsche), and the unconscious (Freud). Vasiliy Kandinsky described the vibe of the 1910s as a time of turning inwards: '[W]hen religion, science and morality are shaken … when the outer supports threaten to fall, man turns his gaze from externals in on to himself. Literature, music and art are the first and most sensitive spheres in which this spiritual revolution makes itself felt.'[10] The spiritual anxiety of this decade, leading up to the First World War, found expression across media. Painters, writers, and musicians were finding new forms to express inner conflicts for which conventional forms were inadequate.[11] Abstract Expressionism, Cubism, Futurism, Dadaism, the 'discovery' of art brut, Serialism in musical composition—all opened new vistas not only into the self but into the soul of a society about to be devastated by war.

If the tension between harmony and dissonance, conservatory and modernist, noise and signal, is like a pendulum, this pendulum swung far to the right in 1937, when, I would argue, the ultimate pro-conservatory, pro-naturalism, pro-mediocrity, anti-noise statement of all time was made: Entartete Kunst [Degenerate Art]. At this exhibit, mounted by the Nazis in Munich, 650 works from the abovementioned Modernist movements were shown to the German (and later Austrian) viewers to warn of the social danger of turning away from naturalism, harmony, and order. A second show, Die Große Deutsche Kunstausstellung [The Great German Art Exhibit], was launched in parallel to showcase 'approved' German art—mostly orderly and anatomically correct sculpture in the Greek and Roman styles, bucolic landscapes, studies of German peasantry.[12] At the opening of Große Deutsche, Hitler himself introduced the war against the avant-garde:

> From now on we will wage a relentless war of cleansing against the last elements of our cultural disintegration. Should there be someone among [the artists] who still believes in his higher destiny—well now, he has had four years' time to prove himself. These four years are sufficient for us to reach a definite judgment. From now on—of that you can be certain—all those mutually supporting and thereby sustaining cliques of chatterers, dilettantes, and art forgers

will be picked up and liquidated. For all we care, those prehistoric Stone-Age culture-barbarians and art-stutterers can return to the caves of their ancestors and there can apply their primitive international scratchings.[13]

This is an environment that hardly would have tolerated Pratella, Stravinsky, Varèse, Schönberg, Xenakis, or anything of the sort. And in fact, specifically didn't. As Entartete Kunst traveled around Germany and Austria, certain iterations were paired with another exhibit entitled Entartete Musik, at which visitors were invited to review the 'degenerate tonality' of Stravinsky and Schönberg, along with Berg, Hindemith, Webern, and more, via German-made headphones. Meanwhile, at the 1936 Summer Olympics in Berlin, Carl Orff's anthemic music served as a soundtrack to the pageantry. Hitler's disparagement of the 'prehistoric' and 'Stone Age' tendencies of Expressionism and Serialism is all the more interesting thinking back to Russolo's observation that music in the post-Industrial age would be dissonant, whereas human life in pre-machine history was quiet.

Which brings us back to noise. The National Socialist approach to 'degenerate music' was supposed to help foster a national (as opposed to 'international') culture and a sense of social hygiene among Germans. Noise in this sense is what you don't like or think shouldn't exist, and part of a worldview that anything in excess of Classicism and realism constitutes a threat to civilization. Whereas in physical systems, such as architecture or electronics, signals are carriers of information, and noise is defined as the interruption of signals, or their absence: white noise on televisions, for example. Simple enough. And yet white noise, guitar feedback, and other so-called interruptions of signal are used expressively, even in popular music. In this sense, then, 'noise' isn't an interruption, but rather a signal that National Socialism—and my friends, apparently—don't like: 'This is noise' / 'It sounds like a boiler room' / 'A rusty train in slow motion.' What does noise mean when it's both signal and absence of signal?

What did noise mean for Russolo in 1913? He apparently was using the term in two different ways: first as the use of dissonance, new timbres, and non-musical, non-metrical sounds in conventional composition and second, as sounds that have no tonal or semantic value. It's unclear, at least to me, whether he drew a distinction between the two.

What does noise mean to my friends for whom I played Iannis Xenakis's *Persepolis*?

If *Le Sacre du Printemps* and *Hyperprism* sound conventional enough today to be played alongside Bach on mainstream Classical music radio, what might *Persepolis* sound like to people in 500 years? Will it, or music by self-identifying 'noise' artists like The New Blockaders and Incapacitants, come to sound like conservatory music over the centuries? Economic theorist Jacques Attali might nod in assent,[14] but I'm not so sure.

In January 1957, Xenakis began work on *Diamorphoses*, his first piece executed entirely on magnetic tape, at Pierre Schaeffer's Le Club d'Essai in Paris. His basic objective for this piece was

> to mix timbres in order to arrive at a body of sound like white noise; to study the evolution of timbres, dynamics and register; to make unisons with attacks only with or without transposition: to make chromosomes of attacks.[15]

His sound sources (or *objets sonores* as he called them) for *Diamorphoses* included 'jets taking off, earthquakes, crashing railroad cars, as well as musical instruments such as bells, percussion and winds.'[16] Not far from 'boiler room' and 'rusty train in slow motion,' actually. But this was 1957. The use of found sounds in composition was only a few years old. What was behind the use of such heavy tonalities in the work? Xenakis was ever exploratory in his approach to music. He didn't know what the contrasts would produce and what new sorts of timbres would result. But with him there was also a greater motivating force than following the trail of pure sound in the studio.

Three years earlier, in the autumn of 1954, Edgard Varèse came to Paris for the premiere of his work *Déserts*. Xenakis was invited to attend rehearsals at the Théâtre des Champs-Elysées. He was excited by Varèse's techniques. He wrote in his diary, 'Extremely interesting the sounds of Varèse, the tension, the roar of intensity—elements of a dynamic technique.'[17] On the night of the premiere, December 2, instead of attending, Xenakis stayed home to record the radio broadcast, in order to study it. Had he attended the premiere he would have witnessed yet another near-riot—in the very same venue where *Le Sacre du Printemps* had been ill-received some four decades before. Even from home Xenakis could hear the jeering: 'Salaud! Pendez-le!'[18] When Varèse visited Xenakis and heard the recording played back, '[a]t the end of the piece, as the uproar led to pandemonium, he broke down and wept.'[19] At the same meeting in Xenakis's Paris hotel room, he showed Varèse a score of his work *Metastaseis*, his first major work, for three percussionists playing seven instruments, twelve wind and forty-six string players, yet lasting only eight minutes. Despite Varèse's aversion for strings he encouraged Xenakis, saying it was 'definitely a music of our time.'[20] So much 'of our time' that after the premiere of *Metastaseis* in 1955 at the Donaueschinger Musiktage, Xenakis was, like Varèse, Stravinsky, and Pratella before him, jeered by the audience who thought the work sounded like noise. As a result, he had to wait four years before his work was allowed to be performed in Paris.[21]

With *Metastaseis*, Xenakis combined elements never before seen in music: architectural mathematics, space time theory, and the acoustics of combat warfare. His driving concern was expanding music's one-dimensional (i.e., linear) and unidirectional form into a relativistic experience of time more like Einstein's: a function of matter and energy. Therefore, register and density become more important in the scoring than tempo, theme, and phrasing. The initial sketches for *Metastaseis* looks more like a blueprint, with masses, surfaces, and ruled lines representing pitch and glissandi. (The score, as we shall see, ended up serving as the basis for Xenakis's design for the Philips Pavilion).[22] But again, beyond music theory and physical systems, there was another motivation behind *Metastaseis*: Xenakis's memories of Occupied Athens during the Second World War, when he fought the Nazis:

> Athens—an anti-Nazi demonstration—hundreds of thousands of people chanting a slogan which reproduces itself like a gigantic rhythm. Then combat with the enemy. The rhythm bursts into an enormous chaos of sharp sounds; the whistling of bullets; the crackling of machine guns. The sounds begin to disperse. Slowly silence falls back on the town. Taken uniquely from an aural point of view and detached from any other aspect these sound events made out of a large number of individual sounds are not separately perceptible, but reunite them again and a new sound is formed which may be perceived in its entirety. It is the same case with the song of the cicadas or the sound of hail or rain, the crashing of waves on the cliffs, the hiss of rain on shingle.[23]

Somewhere along the line it dawned on Xenakis that the total sound of that anti-Nazi demonstration, as he experienced it, was actually thousands of isolatable sounds, a cloud of microsounds distributed in 3D space—the sounds themselves being 'people's shouts and screams, machine-gun fire, rhythmic chanting … a huge choreography whose movement in space, constantly altering in mixture and proportion, which produced a unique composite living sound.'[24] Furthermore, the sequence of the individual shouts and gunshots was irrelevant—unlike themes and phrasing in music, where order is paramount, the elements of the noise of warfare could be arranged in any order and still produce the same result. With this in mind, in *Metastaseis*, the pitch and duration of each of the sixty-five parts of the orchestra are tightly controlled by means of an expanding Fibonacci set. And the result, to hear, is a sound-mass, carefully avalanching, and also containing a central section whose solo instrumentation briefly follows a melodic theme.

Persepolis, the subject of this book, is, like *Metastaseis*, a dense, layered sound construction. Although the structure of *Persepolis* has more in common with other of Xenakis's works, the driving concerns and personal struggles and musical theories are the same. That *Persepolis* would take Xenakis to the deserts of Iran makes this album a story worth recounting at length. If one thing at least should be evident by the end of this book: given its layers of meaning—Xenakis's memories from Athens with the Resistance, with whom he engaged in direct combat with the same ideological forces that sought to erase Modernism in music and art; his application of architectural mathematics and precise spatial sensibilities to his work; his presence on the ground floor of *musique concrète* and the first electronic music studios; the fact that this work premiered in association with what was to be Iran's giant step into Modernity, but which turned out to be part of the story of the Shah's ruin and Iran's turn to theocracy and isolation—despite its possible resemblance to a boiler room or a rusty train in slow motion, *Persepolis* is anything but noise.

Aram Yardumian
Gyumri, Armenia
August 2021

1 The Voice of the Resistance

'In my music,' composer Iannis Xenakis once said, 'there is all the agony of my youth, of the Resistance and the aesthetic problems they posed with the huge street demonstrations, or even more the occasional mysterious, deathly sounds of those cold nights of December '44 in Athens. From this was born my conception of the massing of sound events, and therefore of stochastic music.'[1]

With this statement we can begin looking into the mind that created *Persepolis*, an hour-long piece for electronic tape. Listening to it today, in the wake of scores of other sound-mass albums,[2] it can be difficult to feel the creeping density and architectural precision of *Persepolis* as it would have been heard in 1971, especially at its premiere in the desert landscape of southwest Iran. Of all the elements that come together in this album, however, Xenakis's personal history with the Resistance and memories of Occupied Athens are among the most intriguing.

Xenakis was born in Brăila, an eastern Romanian port city on the Danube, where for centuries Greek and Jewish merchants had controlled the shipping lanes. His birthdate is usually given as May 29, 1922 (though it could be '21; his birth certificate was lost during the war). Brăila is not so far from the Black Sea, which in turn is not so far from the Pontus and the Caucasus, the Levant, and Iran. Though Xenakis learned English, German, and French at home from his family's governesses, culturally he was positioned at the gate of the East.[3] The Xenakis name is common on Crete and likely spread from there across the Aegean Islands and Peloponnese to Izmir (Turkey), where it is also known. Xenakis's paternal great-grandfather was born on Naxos, his grandfather on Euboea, but the family is thought to have come from Crete.[4] His father, Klearchos, as a young man had wished to study theology in Constantinople, but instead was forced to contribute to the family's import-export business. As the eldest child, Klearchos was compelled to finance his younger brothers' educations and contribute to his younger sisters' dowries. He had left Romania in 1912 for Greece to fight the Turks, returning to his business at an unknown later date.[5] Xenakis's mother, Photini, died of measles complications while giving birth to a stillborn girl when Iannis was five. In his few memories of her she is seated at the piano.[6]

At age ten, Xenakis was sent alone to an elite boys' academy called the Anargyrios & Korgialenios School of Spetses. John Fowles would teach at this school after the war. Boys from all over the Greek diaspora were sent to this Greek-English school. Xenakis was among those who did not speak with an Athenian accent and who were shunned by those boys who did. He spent his days in the library reading Victor Hugo, Pindar, Sappho, and books on astronomy. He excelled in sport and academically, though he often favored his own personal reading over schoolwork. He also rekindled an interest in music thanks to an English headmaster named Esmeade Noël Paton, who had gramophone recordings of the European composers.[7] It was from Noël Paton's gramophone that he first 'heard the fifth symphony of Beethoven, which struck me like an apocalypse. From then I entered progressively into music. By listening to it.'[8]

Although these years were lonely and sometimes miserable for Xenakis, they were at least peaceful. Greece had not enjoyed a stable government since before the First World War, and several military coups and rigged elections had ensued, with the usual political groups (socialists, monarchists, Venizelists) vying for power. But in 1936, a fateful decision was made: General Ioannis Metaxas dissolved the Greek parliament and its constitution and imposed a backward-looking authoritarian state modeled with borrowings from Nazi Germany.[9] As Arthur Koestler noted, even Plato's *Republic* was on the list of banned books.[10] Although the Fascist-leaning Metaxas would ultimately side with the Allies in the war to come, his flirtations with Italy and Germany aroused the ire of Athenian students and Venizelists around the country.[11]

It was in a highly politically charged Athens that Xenakis arrived in 1938, only a year before the invasion of Poland and the start of the Second World War (**Figure 1**). Xenakis enrolled in a prep school to pass entrance exams for the prestigious Athens Polytechnic, where he planned to study engineering. For two years, as central and eastern Europe began to crumble, he studied math, physics, and ancient literature, as well as piano, until he met a Soviet-trained Greek composer Aristotelis Koundouroff, in whose classes he learned some harmony and counterpoint. More important, according to Xenakis, Koundouroff impressed upon him what you might call a Russian style of rigor and discipline in composition. To this end, he had Xenakis learn each individual vocal part of Mozart's *Requiem*.[12] At the same time he rekindled an old interest in archeology and rode out to the sites. About this time in his life, he wrote, 'I would ride a bicycle to Marathon. At the supposed place of the battle there was a tumulus with a bas-relief of Aristocles (a/k/a Plato), and I would stay there

Figure 1 *Iannis Xenakis in Athens, c. 1938.*

for long periods, to impregnate myself with the sounds of nature, the crickets and the sea.'[13]

    The year 1940 was a fateful one for Xenakis and for Greece. He passed his Polytechnic exams and was set to enter the university, but just as classes were beginning, Italy invaded Greece from the west. Wartime conditions ensued and the university was forced to close. Six months later, in April 1941, Nazi Germany crossed the border from Yugoslavia and took Thessaloniki. With this strategically crucial port city in German hands, and the forcing of both the Greek Army and Allied forces to surrender, the Axis occupation of Greece began. Extortionate taxes were levied by the Germans and Italians, and as winter set in, famine followed.[14] Xenakis joined the Resistance. At first, he aligned with a right-wing nationalist group, if only because they were better armed and organized, but he later switched to the Communists. '[At first] we organized meetings and demonstrations—that was all. The movement was a rather superficial sort of resistance.'[15] Xenakis wrote little during his lifetime about his personal responsibilities to the Resistance, but he is remembered for having aggressively faced Greek collaborators with the Nazis. 'We organized huge mass demonstrations against the Nazis,' he said, 'with hundreds of thousands of people in the streets. Nowhere else in Europe did you have popular demonstrations on such a scale.'[16]

A man so immersed in ancient philosophy and daily politics, Xenakis found the two could not be kept apart. At the time, he wrote, 'I was reading Plato. I became a Marxist from him. Marx's books did not seem very well written to me, but they represented the only near-contemporary search for harmony within mankind, as well as harmony of mankind and nature as a single whole.'[17] Really what he was doing, he saw in retrospect, was striving to put 'into practice Platonic ideas through Marxist tactics.'[18] The struggle of the Resistance was not only political; it was existential. He had gone from a bookish, marginalized schoolboy to a political figurehead, making public speeches and forming groups and cells of student resistance against the Axis.

The demonstrations in Athens increased through 1942, a year in which, still, the end of the war was unforeseeable. That year the Resistance successfully united a majority of Athenians, and then spread into the countryside. But strife within and between the resistance groups was also growing and would later have a devastating effect, for Churchill, though he found the resistance useful, had no intentions of allowing a Stalinist-Communist state to emerge in southern Europe. Nor did the Nazis. They and their collaborators began deploying armed ultra-nationalist gangs to degrade the Communist groups and disrupt the resistance of the National Liberation Front (EAM) and its armed wing, the Greek People's Liberation Army (ELAS), which were strongly Leftist initiatives.[19]

Then, on February 27, 1943, just weeks after Hitler's defeat by the Red Army at Stalingrad, German radio in Athens announced the 'civil mobilization' of all Greek men aged sixteen to forty-five, threatening deportation to forced labor camps in Nazi Germany.[20] Xenakis was among those who organized the colossal demonstrations against this initiative (**Figure 2**), so successfully that the Germans were forced to cancel the conscription, making Greece the only place in Occupied Europe where the Nazis were unable to implement forced labor.[21] The same year he joined a student resistance group called the United Panhellenic Organization of Youth (EPON), which was a subbranch of the ELAS, and was appointed an officer of the 'Lord Byron' brigade.[22] In the more sympathetic accounts of the Resistance, the Lord Byron battalion is considered among the most heroic. Certainly, they were among those who faced the aggressors head-on. Thanks to the efforts of the ELAS, Italy capitulated in July 1943 and Germany began its own withdrawal in October 1944.

But the fighting was only just beginning. On October 13, 1944, just days after the German evacuation, British troops entered Athens. The supposed liberators were met with joy in the streets. Little did the Resistance fighters and the civil

Figure 2 *A wartime demonstration in Athens, 1930s. Xenakis is second from left.*

population know that the liberating British officers would soon help break the spine of the EAM and destroy any chance of a Leftist government in Greece.[23] Xenakis counts himself among those fooled by the ecstasy of liberation: 'We received them as our allies, as comrades-in-arms … We did not see through the intentions of the British politicians.'[24] The British Commander's order to the ELAS to surrender their arms was met with such disbelief that negotiations failed, demonstrations led to bloodshed, and the infamous *Dekemvriana* ('December Events') began.[25]

RAF planes were buzzing low over the rooftops and British sentries armed with machine guns were stationed in the neighborhoods. To make matters worse, now the Greek right-wing militias were also involved in the conflict, firing on unarmed Athenians. The Resistance continued to fight, but without effective leadership. 'I fought against the English,'

Xenakis wrote, 'who had demanded that the liberation forces lay down their arms. The English bombed the city with their fleet and air force, and they even installed canons at the Acropolis, something the Germans hadn't dared to do.'[26] Xenakis recalled to Nouritza Matossian the story of the day he lost an eye and was nearly killed during a *Dekemvriana* battle in Athens:

> I was with three people inside [a] building. We heard mortars firing and there must have been an explosion that hit us. Two of the people, one a girl, died instantly. One had his brains scattered on the wall. I fell unconscious. After a while they carried me with a white flag to another building which served as a temporary medical post. I heard them say, 'He has only a few hours to live. At least let him die in peace.' And they gave me some shots for the pain, no first aid or precautions against infection; nothing. But I didn't die. When I came around my girlfriend,[27] Mâkhi, another student fighter, was holding my hand; somehow she had managed to find me there. At last I was really happy because I thought I was going to die. That night our side retreated. The next day the British and the collaborators, the National Guard arrived. We had been abandoned, left in the hands of the enemy. I began to swear and shout at them. At least I thought I was swearing but my mouth … ah … a catastrophe. My palate was pierced, there were bits of teeth, flesh, blood, holes, my jawbone was broken. My left eye had burst. I was choking on my own blood and vomiting … anyhow … they left us in there for some hours, then they returned and took me to a central hospital in Athens—instead of killing me. I still did not want to live. My girlfriend was there and after they had operated [on] me to remove the piece of shrapnel which had lodged in my face—it was a big piece—she saved it. Then she went up [to] the mountains and managed to lose it.[28]

It was, as he said, the agony and aesthetics of this period that drove Xenakis to compose. 'Even before the end of the war,' he wrote, 'I had decided, in my distress, to compose music. This alone could help me regain a little calm.'[29] During the war he noticed one of his comrades, a young Communist named Nikos, constantly scribbling musical notation, even during times of jeopardy. They sometimes went out knocking on strangers' doors to ask if there was a piano in the house Nikos could use for a short while. It was through Nikos that Xenakis first heard Bartók, Debussy, and Ravel, and through this, even in at the apex of the conflict, he was able to look into the future. 'I thought peace would come; everything would go back to normal and I would drop politics and study music, which is what I decided I really wanted to do after all.'[30]

Xenakis's hope for a peaceful life of musical composition in Athens was not only a distant hope, it was never to be. When he was discharged from the hospital in March 1945, the Resistance was in retreat, and one year later a far-right government would come to power, leading into the crucial third stage of the Greek Civil War. He returned to the Polytechnic and completed his coursework while continuing to support the waning Resistance. The result of the March 1946 elections was a victory for the United Alignment of Nationalists, an alliance whose supporters had actively terrorized members of the EAM-ELAS and suppressed their votes. The remainder of the Resistance— those who were not killed or forced to take refuge—was conscripted into the regular Greek Army. Those who did not flee to the mountains of Yugoslavia to join General Markos's Democratic Army, or go deep underground in Athens, were forced to bear arms against their comrades.[31]

Xenakis joined the army anticipating his wounds would achieve him an immediate discharge, but instead they assigned him a clerical post. Certain that his record as a Resistance fighter would be found out, his anxiety rose. Indeed, one of the Fascist officers recognized him and ordered him to sign a paper recanting his beliefs or be sent to the notorious concentration camp on Makronisos. 'I refused to sign,' he said.

> Immediately I asked the Commander for leave so that I might seek my father's advice. He granted it and I left the camp as fast as I could. I never set foot in it again. In Athens I went underground. My father was able to pay people to keep me hidden but they were always trying to blackmail him for more money. He was already borrowing at fifty percent interest to support us.[32]

Throughout 1947 Xenakis hid. While in hiding he learned that a military tribunal had sentenced him to death for desertion. During the war years, free citizens were not granted exit visas. But there was a loophole: the Dodecanese islands, an Italian possession from 1912 to 1947, were formally united with Greece by a peace treaty signed in February of that year but which did not come into full effect until September.[33] Between those months, it seems, Dodecanese Greeks maintained their 'Italian' privileges, which included traveling to Italy without a visa, and from Italy one could slip into Europe. Xenakis's father arranged a forged Dodecanese passport for his son and in September of that year, he departed Greece as Konstantin Kastrounis.[34] With the sounds of the demonstrations and gunfire still echoing in his head, Xenakis left Greece, not to return for three decades.[35]

2 Paris, 1947

Xenakis arrived in Paris in a moment when it was hardly in better shape than the Athens he had left behind. Although it had escaped the ruination of London, Frampol, Rotterdam, and the bombed-out German cities, the outer suburbs and communes that form a ring around Paris, and certain inner *arrondissements*—especially the factory areas—were hit hard.[1] Partisan tensions continued to flare and even in 1947 food shortages were a daily struggle all over France.[2] But already, famous writers and artists were walking the newly liberated streets and reading newspapers in the cafés. Culturally, Paris was picking up where it had left before the rude interruption of the Nazi Occupation and the État français. Sartre and de Beauvoir were back to holding court in the cafés of Saint-Germain-des-Prés. Ernest Hemingway and Gertrude Stein, the torchbearers of the pre-War literary scene, made their brief returns. French composers such as Darius Milhaud and Arthur Honegger continued their Neoclassical work. The jazz clubs were back to capacity, and the art galleries were booming with Surrealist and geometric abstractionist work, as well as retrospectives of Van Gogh, as if the war had never happened. But there was also something new in the air. A new sensibility was emerging from the unlikeliest of places—the radio studio—and with the unlikeliest of technologies—a wartime development called magnetic tape.

With his cardboard suitcase, Xenakis had made his way from the Dodecanese Islands to the French Consul in Rome.[3] The consulate looked sideways at his obviously forged passport and directed him to the Greek Embassy. Xenakis knew going there would be tantamount to suicide, so he instead contacted representatives of the Communist Party, who arranged for his passage from Turin to Paris, illegally, with the help of a Communist frontier guard.[4] He arrived in Paris on November 11, 1947, in the midst of a general strike that was quickly spreading across the country, and some feared a civil war would soon break out. All essential services had been suspended. Xenakis remembers that 'there was no food, terribly poverty, and unemployment.' Having just come from similar conditions in Greece, he 'was disappointed and frightened. All I saw was dust and ruins.'[5] In fact, he had no intention of staying in Paris, but rather only moving through in transit to the United States, where his brother Jason was studying philosophy, and where he, Iannis, dreamed of studying 'astrophysics, mathematics, archeology and music.'[6]

His Communist contacts, perhaps too busy with the general strike, were unable to help him secure employment. Thus, he had only one card to play: his diploma of engineering from the Polytechnic. With this, and a great deal of luck, he managed to secure a low-level position at the firm of Swiss-French architect Le Corbusier, one of the pioneers of modern architecture. Xenakis had never heard of Le Corbusier and at first, apparently, did not realize how fortunate he was. At the time, Le Corbusier, entering the final stage of his career, was at work on what he called his 'Parthenon,' the Unité d'habitation de Marseille, a 340-unit modernist housing unit in the southern French port city. Xenakis was assigned the task of calculating the structural load of the slabs and floors.[7]

In 1950, at a dinner organized by a friend, Xenakis met a young, quiet woman, another child of war—one who, like Xenakis, had been hunted for aiding the Resistance. Three years later he and Françoise Gargouïl were married, and they settled into a life together in a Parisian apartment so small that when one was at the desk the other was confined to the bed. It was also at this time that Xenakis was beginning to think more seriously about music as public expression, not just a private universe, and Françoise recollects her husband composing far into the nights. Aware of his limitations as far as musical education, but also of his own refusal to go the traditional conservatory route, Xenakis sought out instruction with Darius Milhaud and Arthur Honegger. This went nowhere. His interview with Honegger was especially disastrous.[8] In 1951, Le Corbusier, who pretended to dislike music,[9] was nevertheless insightful enough to recognize that two French composers of the era were worth paying attention to: Edgard Varèse and Olivier Messiaen.

Neither Varèse nor Messiaen fit the mold of the post-War French Neo-Classical revival, though for very different reasons, the former for having freed himself from linear themes and rhythms, and the latter for his use of predetermined pitches (not to mention strong religious and mystical themes). Xenakis approached Messiaen after a lecture one day in 1951 and immediately the two understood each other. Messiaen, who still believed very much in learning harmony and counterpoint, saw that Xenakis was not a typical student:

> I asked him many questions. First of all he impressed me physically, because he carries those great scars, those glorious wounds. He is of superior intelligence. I learned that he was Greek, an architect and worked with Le Corbusier, that he did special mathematics…. this was a man so much

out of the ordinary that I said, 'No, you are almost thirty, you have the good fortune of being Greek, of being an architect and having studied special mathematics. Take advantage of these things. Do them in your music.'[10]

Xenakis had introduced himself to Messiaen at a low and discouraged point, but after the meeting he began to compose with a renewed confidence. Inspired by Messiaen's free mind, his strict adherence to his own rules, Xenakis began thinking more about the problem of physical space in music: in architecture, physical space may be entered into, crossed and re-crossed, but time in music is linear and irreversible. 'During this period,' Xenakis wrote, 'I felt strongly the link that is often made between music and architecture, and their respective influences on me were fundamental.'[11] Already he was mentally constructing his first musical scores, starting with piano and vocal works, some of which date to 1949. More notably, he composed a four-hand piano piece called *Zyia Kathisto* (1952), a choral-instrumental piece called *Anastenaria* (1952–3). His first published work, *Metastaseis* (1954), was something else altogether.

Metastaseis is the first piece of music in which we can hear—and see—Xenakis's vision of music as architecture. In 1953, he asked Le Corbusier for an opportunity to design something on his own. 'He accepted,' Xenakis remembers, 'and entrusted me with the project of the convent at Tourette in Éveux-sur l'Arbresle [1954–60]. I helped draw up all the plans for the convent, but the final result is a mix of my ideas and Le Corbusier's.'[12] This was to be Xenakis's first serious collaboration in architectural design, whereas his involvement before the Couvent was mostly limited to calculating resistance in building materials such as concrete. At the same time he was also beginning to compose *Metastaseis*.

His initial studies for this work were not, however, laid out in formal notation, but rather ruled parabolas, on graph paper (**Figure 3**). Each of the forty-six ruled lines of the parabola represented the unfolding of simultaneous glissandi, starting from a single point. Musically, this would mean forty-six string instruments beginning with a single pitch (G) and gradually unfolding geometrically, like the parabola, with each member of the string section initiating a gradual change in direction until they, joined by horns and trombones, arrive at a sound mass that spans several octaves. There is no discernible meter in the piece—even the rhythmic pattern of the woodblock seems to derive from the Fibonacci series.

Xenakis believed that music as a phenomenon followed the same laws as the rest of the universe, and the theory attributed to the Pythagoreans that 'all things are numbers.'[13] This tenet, he maintained, was still adhered to among engineers, physicists,

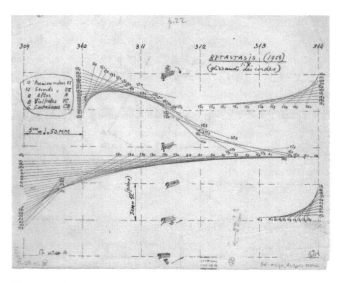

Figure 3 Metastaseis 'score' (1954).

economists, and so on, but had somewhere along the way vanished from the sphere of music. In the liner notes to the 1967 Vanguard edition of *Metastasis/Pithoprakta/Eonta* (VCS-10030),[14] he recommends advancing music to the point where it can 'guide physics and mathematics again, as in the days of its Pythagorean birth.'[15]

In *Metastaseis*, the progression of musical integers follows the Fibonacci series, whose successive terms express the golden ratio. In Le Corbusier's *atelier*, a system of 'harmonious measurements' called the Modulor was used. This complex anthropomorphic scale of proportion, combining human measurements with the Golden Mean and Fibonacci numbers, was, Le Corbusier seemed to think, as fundamental to the order of nature as meters and feet.[16] Xenakis's design for the windows of the Couvent also followed Modulor measurements, producing panels of various widths, the intervals of which produced a rhythm for the eye.

The first section of *Metastaseis*, following the culmination of the sound mass, ends rather abruptly and becomes a work for strings, brass, and woodwinds, with some percussion. The texture builds upon a ten-note set in serialist fashion, with the occasional use of tremolo before entering a third section with even more instruments and a stronger and more complex rhythmic element. Finally, the piece concludes with another string glissando, this time beginning with the sound mass and unraveling back to the same single pitch with which the piece began (although, as James Harley points out, it is a G# this time, not a G).[17]

Xenakis considered the mathematics he employed in such compositions to be an application of stochastic theory, not probability per se, because, as he notes, stochastic processes govern 'asymmetry, symmetry, [densities, degrees of order and disorder], the individual, the mass, as no other method does.'[18] This is an important distinction, since stochastic music encompasses both determined and indeterminate changes.

The title, *Metastaseis*, translates from the Greek as 'beyond + stasis.' In singular form it is a word that most non-Hellenophones know from cancer diagnostics—a word you never, ever want to hear. But in this case, the title reflects Xenakis's belief that both chromatic tonalism and serialism were static when compared with the infinite number of sounds offered by physics and mathematics. *Metastaseis* is not Free Music in the sense that there is no structure; on the contrary, the music is like a cell continuously permutating in 3D space, hence metastasis. Historically, the importance of this 1954 work is found in Xenakis's attempt to build an entirely new approach to music, one neither tonal nor atonal, but an altogether new direction. It served as the inauguration of the concept of the sound-mass, a conception that Xenakis would expand upon for the rest of his life. All this in a piece that lasts only eight minutes.

As mentioned in this book's Introduction, the premiere of *Metastaseis* at the Donaueschinger Musiktage in 1955 divided the audience. Some, like Heinrich Strobel, the festival organizer, praised the work, albeit in empirical terms: 'It is an atomic music.'[19] Others, like Antoine Goléa, the chairman of a conference on the future of music, which was held at the festival, despised *Metastaseis*, writing that this 'protoplasm-like material was devoid of any interest.'[20] While half the audience applauded, the rest jeered. It would be the 'first and last time that a work mine,' Xenakis said, 'received its premiere at those festivals. New music was in the hands of the serialists, who prevented any other trend from making itself heard.'[21] Serialism, only three decades before the vanguard of freedom from constraint, was already a nest of conservatism and resistance to innovation.

But by this time Xenakis had already turned his attention to something new.

3   The Voice of the Avant-garde

It seems obvious to say that life in Europe after the Second World War was never the same. The Reconstruction (and division) of Germany, the Iron Curtain, the EU, the Cold War, decline of colonial investiture, immense loss of life, and so on brought about changes both sudden and creeping. At the same time, the landscape of European life looked very similar after the War as it did in the nineteenth century. As Tony Judt pointed out, in the 1950s, farmers in Belgium still gathered hay with wooden rakes, handpicked fruits and vegetables, and transported them with horses and carts; coal-powered England hung in a kind of 'Edwardian limbo,' by which he means the landscape looked and felt like that of Anthony Asquith's *The Winslow Boy* (1948); and in Spain the Catholic Church had the power to censor under Franco's regressive right-wing regime.[1] All this, while jet engine planes flew overhead guided by radar, while lives were being saved by blood transfusion, and while researchers were busy developing atomic energy, stored-program computers, and unraveling the basis of life in human DNA. In fact, DNA aside, all these technologies directly emerged from, or were hastened by the War. Mainstream artistic life in Europe, on the other hand, seemed to change very little. The pendulum of innovation had swung to New York and few postwar European artists were producing work that reflected these contrasts between traditional lifeways and encroaching Modernity.

Exceptions like Jean Dubuffet, Joseph Beuys, and Peter Weiss aside, most European artists and musicians in the 1940s and early 1950s simply continued with techniques and traditions established before the War, perhaps reflecting a nostalgia for prewar, pre-modern life; perhaps due to a lack of tools and materials; and perhaps because the effects of the devastation took longer to sink in.

In the realm of experimental music, however, things were changing faster thanks to another innovation that emerged directly from wartime technology: magnetic tape. Sound was successfully recorded on magnetized steel wire in the late nineteenth century. In fact, magnetic tape was just a redesigning of this basic idea. In 1927, German engineer Fritz Pfleumer glued pulverized iron particles onto 16 mm strips of paper (the upper 8 mm forward, the lower 8 mm in reverse) and recorded sound on them. He played the tape on a demonstration machine, an open-reel tape recorder which he called the Magnetophon K1. The sound was generally considered poor, but everyone could see the great potential of this technology once improved.[2] The first known recording on the Magnetophon was made on November 19, 1936: Sir Thomas Beecham and the London Philharmonic playing works by Mozart, Rimsky-Korsakov,[3] and Dvořák at the BASF Feierabendhaus in Ludwigshaven. But the sound quality was highly distorted. The real leap in quality came with the change in materials used for the magnetic tape itself: the replacement of Fe_3O_4 oxide tape by γ-Fe_2O_3 with red iron oxide particles.[4] It was 1939 and magnetic tape was now a part of the war effort.

The Magnetophone was a German patent and the improvements (such as AC bias and PVC film-backed tape), made under cover of war, were largely unknown to the Allies. They did know, however, that the Nazis were using some sort of transcription technology because they were hearing identical German radio programs—including speeches by Hitler—cast simultaneously in multiple time zones, but the programs were far too long to be sourced from records, even discs recorded at 16 RPM.[5] Major Jack Mullin, a US Army Signal Corpsman stationed in the UK during the War, listened to late-night classical music concerts on German radio:

> Strauss and Lehar melodies played by a full orchestra—solo arias from Vienese [*sic*] operettas. What? At this hour? More full orchestra—a male chorus singing songs of the Rhine and so on through the night. How could they do it? The sound was so flawless that we were convinced we were hearing live performances. The usual deficiencies of record scratch and other tell-tale distortions were completely absent.[6]

The only way long, undistorted concerts could be broadcast all night, was improved magnetic tape, but what had the Germans done? The mystery was solved during the Allied invasion of September 1944 with the discovery of improved Magnetophones at Radio Luxembourg. The Germans had evidently failed to destroy them there as they had in other radio stations.[7] Mullin himself took possession of some K-4 recorders at a station in Frankfurt-am Main and shipped them home to California. There, he rebuilt the machines and, along with Richard Ranger, his colleague from the Signal Corps, set about demonstrating them to American companies such as Ampex.[8] From there, at the behest of Bing Crosby, further technical improvements were made, resulting in the Ampex Model 200 (which debuted in 1948), which went on to revolutionize the broadcast and recording industries.[9]

In Paris, as early as 1941, a Parisian electroacoustic engineer named Pierre Schaeffer was theorizing about the relationship between the 'broadcast arts' (specifically radio and film) and the instruments of their transmission, meaning, the radio stations, and cinema houses themselves. Schaeffer, who came from a musical family and claimed to have had formal training in theory, piano, and cello, was working for the RTF (Radio Télévision Francais).[10] Whereas music itself was an abstract art, radio programs and film employed concrete images and sounds. Through this he came to the conclusion that radio and cinema could serve as 'relays' between concrete and abstract, and that the use of concrete forms by these media (which he referred to as *arts-relais*) constituted a language unto itself, a *langage des choses* (language of things).[11]

In 1942, Schaeffer and theater director Jacques Copeau established Studio d'Essai (in 1946 renamed Club d'Essai de la Radiodiffusion-Télévision Française), an experimental audio lab, which during the War secretly recorded Resistance radio programs that would not have passed the Nazi censors. The studio was also reputedly the first to broadcast freely upon liberation on August 25, 1944.[12] Over the next few years, Schaeffer continued his radiophonic work at Studio d'Essai. Then, in 1948, he claims to have been struck by the idea to record 'a concert of locomotives.' He took a radio sound truck to the historic Saint-Lazare rail marshalling yard in Batignolles, a neighborhood in the 17th arrondissement, and there recorded the sounds of trains going in and out of the station.[13] These recordings, made by directly cutting shellac discs at 78 RPM,[14] were applied to a sound collage Schaeffer called 'Étude aux chemins de fer' (literally 'study of the tracks of iron,' but better translated as 'Railroad Study'). He composed four other sound collages the same year: 'Étude aux Tourniquets' (a collage of music boxes and zanzis); 'Étude pour Orchestre' (the sounds of an orchestra tuning up); 'Étude au Piano' (piano sounds); and

'Étude aux Casseroles' (sounds of pots and pans in a kitchen). These five sound pieces, collectively called *Cinq etudes de bruits*, were radio broadcast on October 5, 1948, as *Concert de bruits*.[15] This broadcast was the public debut of what Schaeffer would call *musique concrète*.

Against the odds, the broadcast was a great success and provoked enough interest among the Paris music community that Schaeffer began to receive visits and proposals for involvement from local musicians. As a result, he was granted an assistant, twenty-year-old Pierre Henry, a pupil of Messiaen, who, in collaboration with Schaeffer between 1949 and 1957, played a vital role in the shape and sound of *musique concrète* and electronic music.[16] During 1949–50, the two Pierres produced what would be the first longform electroacoustic composition. Titled 'Symphonie Pour Un Homme Seul,' the piece was premiered on March 18, 1950, at the École Normale de Musique de Paris. Those in attendance heard a 'symphony' in eleven short movements of modified sounds (speaking, whistling, breathing, laughing, footsteps) blended together and with orchestral music.[17] Perhaps the crucial strategy employed in this and subsequent pieces was clipping the initial moment of individual sounds, rendering them non-referential, and thereby achieving a kind of artistic purity as opposed to a collage of sound effects.

Very few composers had incorporated sound recordings into their works before Schaeffer and Henry, and those who did left the recordings largely unmodified.[18] That is to say, they didn't reverse them, slow them down and speed them up, alter their pitch and timbre, edit them, or superimpose them over one another in a way that resembled overdubbing, as Schaeffer did at the Club d'Essai. He referred to the individual recorded sounds of *musique concrète* as *objets sonores*. Remarkably, all this was done before the introduction of magnetic tape and electronic studios.[19]

The year 1951 saw the establishment of the Groupe de Recherche de Musique Concrète (GRMC), which later became the Groupe de Recherches Musicales (GRM). Along with it, Schaeffer also established Europe's first electroacoustic music studio.[20] The same year the Studio für elektronische Musik des Westdeutschen Rundfunks in Cologne was established, setting France and Germany on separate courses for production of electronic music.[21] It is important to note that *musique concrète* and *elektronische Musik* weren't the same thing in the 1940s and 1950s. However much they may have merged since then and are indistinguishable now, elektronische Musik, which emerged from the Cologne studio in 1951, was something Schaeffer actively opposed.[22] For him, the distinction was simple: *elektronische Musik* was a systematic approach, through which one could create musical forms through precise control of the oscillators, whereas *musique concrète* was a more experimental approach, and a more empirical one, beginning with the sounds themselves (be they thunder, rain, the creak of a door) and from it a structure emerges.[23] In other words, the most important element in *musique concrète* composition was the sound itself—its timbral and textural qualities. *Elektronische Musik* also made use of found sounds, but the Cologne-based group, which included Karlheinz Stockhausen, Herbert Eimert, and György Ligeti, among others, composed more traditionally, even serially, with purely electronic sounds as well as manipulated found sounds.[24]

Eventually the GRM became the home for an entire era of post-War composers, among them many recognizable names, such as Pierre Boulez, Olivier Messiaen, Edgard Varèse (who used the GRM studios to complete the electronic portions of *Déserts*),

Michel Philippot, Luc Ferrari, Bernard Parmegiani, François Bayle, François-Bernard Mâche, Karlheinz Stockhausen, and, of course, Iannis Xenakis.[25]

Schaeffer, for his part, has admitted in retrospect to being happy about the technical difficulties he overcame, with turntables and early tape recorders, but ultimately was unhappy with what he produced: 'Each time I was to experience the disappointment of not arriving at music. I couldn't get to music—what I call music. I think of myself as an explorer struggling to find a way through in the far north, but I wasn't finding a way through.' After the War he said, we drove 'back the German invasion but we hadn't driven back the invasion of Austrian music, 12-tone music. We had liberated ourselves politically, but music was still under an occupying foreign power, the music of the Vienna school.'[26]

Xenakis, who had also butted heads with serialist composers at Donaueschinger, would surely have agreed with this sentiment to an extent, but his interest in Schaeffer and the GRM was more *concrète*, if you will. In an electroacoustic studio, he understood, he could work with the physical properties of sound in much the same way he worked with the materials of architecture in terms of physics and mathematics. Although his approach seems perfectly suited to *musique concrète* and an electroacoustic studio setting, his initial overtures to Schaeffer went unanswered. Aware that Pierre Henry, Pierre Boulez, and Messiaen were involved, he continued attending GRM concerts and redoubled his efforts 'to show [Schaeffer] that I was a musician and not a wanderer.'[27] Perhaps Schaeffer was aware but simply didn't see the value in Xenakis's material-analytical approach to music. Xenakis sent him the score to his choral work *Anastenaria* (1952–4), but the score was returned without an invitation to visit the studio. Then he telephoned and reached Schaeffer, who said that he did not know about the score, and furthermore could not read music, but that he would have Pierre Henry study it if Messiaen would write a recommendation. Messiaen was willing to write the letter—an act Xenakis described as 'a bomb, a gift. I must have it photographed.'[28]

Xenakis began attending meetings at the Club d'Essai with Schaeffer, Henry, Ferrari, Philippot, and others, with whom he soon became closely acquainted. Around January 1957, he began collecting recordings for a work to be entitled *Diamorphoses*—low-frequency sounds: trains, a jet taking off, and an earthquake; but also some high-register musical sounds like bells and percussion. Some of these would be tape-manipulated to alter the speed, others seem unmanipulated. The effect is one of contrasts between the high and low registers and an unfolding maze of sonorities.[29] Xenakis wrote very little about this seven-minute piece but explained in an interview[30] his interest in the phenomenon of sonic density in this and his other work at the GRM. As an exploration of density, he said, *Diamorphoses* is a layering of shifts and sustained *objets sonores*, for which he calculated a range of activities and 'attack points,' by which is meant the moment the envelope of sound is opened.

The following year he produced a second tape study of sonic density, *Concret PH* (1958), this time a two-and-three-quarters minute miniature whose only sound source was the crackling of a charcoal fire.[31] Xenakis used overdubs and pitch transposition to make the sound glisten, almost as if you are hearing metal fragments being sprinkled on a surface. The piece changes tone at least twice in less than three minutes, possibly as an internal evolution, or possibly as a product of how it would have been heard on a multichannel system in

3D space. Unlike *Diamorphoses*, *Concret PH* was commissioned as the introduction to Varèse's *Poème électronique*, which in turn had been commissioned as an audio installation at the Philips Pavilion at the 1958 Brussels World's Fair (**Figure 4**).

Built by Le Corbusier, the Pavilion was commissioned by Philips 'to demonstrate their capabilities in modern technology of lighting, electroacoustics, automatic control in electronics, and so forth.'[32] Le Corbusier's original vision for the Pavilion was as a giant stomach, with visitors passing through like particles in digestion, accompanied by music and images. Describing his vision in a letter to Varèse, Le Corbusier wrote,

> This interior is plunged into the most complete night. Every eight minutes six or eight hundred people will enter and leave. Therefore an event should arise of eight minutes duration and this play will be of an exclusively "electric" nature […] My idea is that music should have a part in this.[33]

Because the commission arrived while Le Corbusier was absorbed with his design plans for the city of Chandigarh,[34] management of the Philips Pavilion project was assigned to Xenakis. Briefed on Le Corbusier's vision for the Pavilion, Xenakis, now with ten years of experience in architecture behind him, began to let his imagination soar. His mind still reeling from the creation of *Metastaseis*, he began to think about the physical structure of the Pavilion in terms of the paraboloids and glissandi he had used to compose this piece. His sketches of the building's shell hardly reflected Le Corbusier's original vision for a convex shell, but the latter enthusiastically approved them anyway. But then when the Pavilion was built, it was Le Corbusier who turned up to appear in the publicity and take credit for it. Xenakis fought him on it, publicly, and in doing so was fighting a long tradition of master

Figure 4 *The Philips Pavilion, 1958 World's Fair, Brussels.*

architects taking credit for the work of their protégés. Xenakis eventually succeeded and Le Corbusier agreed to allowing Xenakis to appear as co-designer in print.[35]

While all this was going on, Varèse was experiencing his own problems. The tapes for *Poème électronique* had been completed at the Philips studios in Eindhoven, which had been specially outfitted for the multi-channel projection of sound (via 350 or 400 or 425 speakers, accounts vary) in the Pavilion space. But Varèse didn't like the equipment at the studio and in turn the Philips representatives didn't like what he produced. Le Corbusier would not allow Xenakis to travel to the studios in Eindhoven to complete *Concret PH*[36] because his presence was needed in Paris while Le Corbusier, himself, was in Chandigarh for weeks at a time. In the end, the original *Concret PH* for use at the Pavilion was produced at Philips Paris, and later redone at GRM.[37]

The Philips Pavilion really was a remarkable feat of innovation. That it was demolished the year after it was built has made its study purely theoretical, but there has even been talk of permanently reconstructing it.[38] Beyond its bold modernity and its reputation for having prefigured computer-aided design, the Pavilion's nine large concrete hyperbolic paraboloids (in 3D space, a double-curved surface that has contours like a Pringle) appeared almost as different buildings from different angles as visitors moved around. And though such things, while visually stunning, often create impossible tasks for structural engineers, Xenakis's calculations ensured the thin, pre-pressed concrete shell had the capacity to support more than its own weight.[39]

Le Corbusier's vision for *Poème électronique* was far more than the architectural shell of the Pavilion. In fact, Xenakis's parabolic exterior and Le Corbusier's multimedia interior were disconnected experiences—the outside gave no indication of what one would find within. Inside, visitors—who, remember, were to be 'ingested, violently churned and decomposed by the digestive enzyme of the *Poème*, and excreted back to the fairground'[40]—found themselves in a darkened space filled with colored light. On the walls they viewed a montage of photographs and film-stills that depicted an anthropological view of humanity: ritual, fetish objects, masks, expressions of faith, tribal practices and 'primitive' art, the Sphinx, wild animals, war reportage, scientific and technological themes representing Modernity. With this sweeping narrative of civilization, Le Corbusier wished to affirm a common humanity in the atomic age, and the desire for redemption, with a utopian climax: Le Corbusier's own projects, representing architecture's unique propensity to bring order to chaos.[41]

Accompanying this montage was the eight-minute piece for electronic tape by Varèse, for which he used recordings of church bells, gunshots, percussion, voices, choirs, a piano, machines, and synthesized tones. Studio processing at Eindhoven allowed for a complex 'surround sound' effect with the 400-odd speakers.[42] Xenakis's two-minute *Concret PH* served as a kind of palate cleanser between the eight-minute iterations of the *Poème électronique*, allowing the visitors to better ingest the Pavilion and the Pavilion the visitors.

In the end, Xenakis was disappointed with the *Poème électronique* for reasons beyond his conflict with Le Corbusier, which soon would lead to Xenakis's dismissal from the *atelier* in 1959, and what might have been a departure from architecture altogether. The aesthetics of the montage were dissatisfying to him because, as he wrote, 'I thought he was going to do something abstract and this was his opportunity, but he just projected films and slides of realistic events.'[43] In an article published the year after the Brussels World's Fair he developed his ideas further:

> Abstraction is understood to be the conscious manipulation of laws and pure notions, and not of concrete objects. In fact, the play of forms and colors detached from their concrete context implies conceptual relationships of a higher level.[44]

Despite his perception of the *Poème* as a lost opportunity to create a higher, purer art, the entire Philips Pavilion experience would have positive effects on his work for the rest of his life. The total aesthetic experience afforded by the of architecture, imagery, stage lighting, electronic music, time-space interaction, and the possibility of transformation at work in the

Pavilion would inform Xenakis's polytopes, including *Persepolis*, and the crowning *Diatope* (Pompidou Centre, Paris, 1978).

Two years after being sacked, Xenakis met Le Corbusier at the inauguration of the Couvent de la Tourette. The two were cordial and Le Corbusier even asked him to rejoin the firm, but Xenakis replied that it was too late to come back to architecture—all he wanted to do was compose, to write about music and compose.[45]

4   The Voice of Cyrus

Room 52 of the British Museum houses ancient artifacts from across the vast world known as Persia. Far greater than the borders of modern Iran, the Persian Empire at various times incorporated provinces as far east as Pakistan, and to the north the Caucasus and most of what is now called Central Asia. Persia (or Parsa) itself was a small region, roughly the size of today's Fars province in southern Iran. Pasargadae, one of ancient Persia's two capitals, still stands today as a ruin. About fifty miles southwest, along the road to Shiraz, lie the ruins of Achaemenid Persia's second capital, Persepolis.

Among the treasures in Room 52's museum-glass cases there is a model chariot, complete with horses, riders, and reins, all delicately fashioned from gold; a Parthian belt buckle featuring an eagle clasping its prey, possibly a rabbit or a ram, in its claws; and a silver bowl decorated with a *simurgh*—a dog-lion-peacock creature from Zoroastrian mythology. But the most historically important artifact in the room greets you when you enter: a barrel-shaped clay token found at Babylon in 1879, though the cylinder itself dates to the sixth century BCE (**Figure 5**). Only eight inches long, the Akkadian cuneiform text on this small and unassuming object bears a significant message: religious communities within the Achaemenid Empire, under Cyrus the Great, would, allegedly, be granted the freedom to manage their own affairs, and not obligated to follow the traditions of the Persians. Furthermore, the edict has been interpreted as implying permission for the repatriation

Figure 5 *The Cyrus Cylinder, British Museum.*

of exiled peoples and the restoration of temples (though the factuality of this has been disputed).[1]

On Tuesday, October 12, 1971, Mohammed Reza Shah Pahlavi, the last Shah of Iran, stood at the ruins of Pasargadae before a crowd of journalists, academics, and military personnel and inaugurated a celebration marking the 2,500th anniversary of the founding of the Persian Empire (*Jashnehā-ye 2500 Sal-e Shāhanshāhi-ye Iran*). During his speech, he invoked the achievements of Cyrus the Great, the Empire's founder, praising him for having exercised 'the highest human principles of mutual understanding among nations and religious freedom.'[2] The same year the Shah's sister, Princess Ashraf Pahlavi, took this same message, along with a replica of the Cylinder, to the United Nations, saying, 'The heritage of Cyrus was the heritage of human understanding, tolerance, courage, compassion and, above all, human liberty.'[3] The Cylinder 'became the centerpiece of the official logo of the 2500th anniversary Celebrations, which featured the artefact in a blue halo, with the Pahlavi coat of arms above, surrounded by Persepolitan-style flowers.'[4] All officially published literature associated with the event bore its image as a kind of brand. Among this literature was an essay by Belgian linguist Maurice Leroy, who characterized Cyrus's edict as such:

> It is not without reason that the Iranian state authorities have today called this document the First Declaration of Human Rights, since, in a world that is too often ruled by the most implacable cruelties, such a thing sounds fresh, even unusual.[5]

Beyond this, why in 1971, of all years, did everyone suddenly take an interest in a 2,000-year-old Akkadian text that supposedly granted religious freedom to the diverse peoples of the Persian Empire? Why was the Shah implying that Iran, of all places, could serve as a beacon of freedom and tolerance in the world?

All this attention paid to the Cyrus Cylinder and other throwbacks to an ancient, more tolerant pre-Islamic Persia were part of a build-up to Iran's emergence as a power on the world stage. The 2,500th anniversary celebration would showcase both Iran's ancient history and its recent advances as a modern state. The peak of the weeklong event (October 12– 16, 1971) was to be the grandest and most expensive banquet the world had ever known, followed by an elaborate *son et lumière* show at the Persepolis ruin. According to the invitation literature Xenakis received,

> To mark twenty-five centuries of continuous existence as a national entity and to honour the memory of Cyrus-the-Great who was the first to formulate the inalienable rights of man, IRAN will assemble together more than fifty Heads of State and foreign dignitaries from all geographical and political horizons of the world, at the very steps of the ruins of the ancient capital of the Achaemenid Kings.[6]

A month and a half earlier, beginning on August 26, at the Fifth Annual Shiraz Arts Festival, Iannis Xenakis premiered his electroacoustic work *Persepolis* in the same ancient urban landscape, thus cementing his connection with the fateful yearlong celebrations of 1971.[7]

It may be disconcerting to hear the Shah's promise for a humanistic and tolerant Iran, as it never came to pass. Instead, eight years later he and his family would flee the country, never to return, and the Ayatollah Khomeini would arrive, altering the course of world history forever. It is all the more significant, then, that the Shah chose Cyrus the Great as a symbol for Iran's past and future. Cyrus (whose name was probably pronounced more like 'Kourosh') was among the greatest imperialists in history, expanding his influence throughout the Middle East during his reign (559–530 BCE), but he also had a reputation for benevolence. Historians of Jewish tradition see the edict of Cyrus as corroboration of the biblical tradition of the release of the Israelites from Babylonian captivity by Cyrus (as in Ezra and 2 Chronicles).[8]

If Mohammad Reza Pahlavi sought to portray himself as the spiritual successor to Cyrus, as Alexander the Great had done, to further authenticate and legitimize his rule, he did so neither in a historical vacuum nor as a reactionary conservative. On the contrary, even in the nineteenth century, Persian intellectuals were criticizing the role of Islam in public life and proposing a more secular vision for the nation, based on their readings of Renan, Montesquieu, and Voltaire.[9]

The Persian past served as the perfect template for recasting Iran's nationhood and tolerance and creating a sense of continuity from ancient to modern. This was because of both how much was known about ancient Persia, and how little. Some Qajar historians even attempted to connect the 'modernity and authenticity' of ancient Persia to that of modern Persia, with a period of Islamic backwardness in between.[10]

Unsurprisingly, the rise of national self-consciousness in nineteenth-century Iran had a mirror in Europe, and that mirror was called Aryanism. The same Aryanism that gave rise—via Gobineau and Chamberlain (and arguably Wagner)—to the notion of *Herrenvolk* and the danger of Jewish blood had a less virulent sister theory in Iran. Aryan and Iran are, after all, the same word. But Aryanism in Iran was not anti-Jewish and did not denote a racial hierarchy per se. Instead, it sought to reawaken what was seen as the 'Aryan heritage' of ancient Persia—the 'glories of the Achaemenid and Sasanian periods in their search for the real Persia, a Persia uncontaminated by foreign culture and customs, one which commanded respect from the world.'[11] After a certain point there was another aspect to this resurgent Aryanism: to foster closer relations with Europe by convincing Europeans that they and Persians belonged to the same race. As the Shah intimated to Oriana Fallaci in a 1970s interview:

> No, we Iranians aren't all that different from you Europeans. If our women wear the veil, so do yours. The veil of the Catholic Church. If our men have more than one wife, so do yours. The wives you call mistresses. And if we believe in visions, you believe in dogmas. If you think yourselves superior, we have no complexes. Don't ever forget that whatever you have, we taught you three thousand years ago.[12]

Even if some of this rhetoric feels a bit strained (as does the entire interview if you read all of it), the meaning is clear: Iran was to be a cultured and civilized nation of equal standing to Europe, one speaking an Indo-European classical language related to Greek, Italian, French, and English. And furthermore, Iran was (so the theory went) the original home of the Aryans, the racial stock 'from whom most Americans and Europeans are descended.'[13] Even if these linguistic and racial notions of European 'origins' in Persia are quaint at best, and his disparagement of Arabs and Arab culture a bit resentful, the Shah was right to point out that Persia was not Arabia and Persians were not Arabs (even today this distinction has to be made routinely), and the only real tie between the two was Islam, something the Shah did not wish to discard outright, but where he saw clerical backwardness in Egypt and Saudi Arabia, he, like his father before him, saw a great potential for a progressive Iran dominating the region. Instead, Iran should be transformed from a stagnant Islamic backwater into a modern, industrial, European-leaning, and perhaps even secular state.

Attendant to these concerns, Iran underwent a series of modernizing reforms in the twentieth century. Under Reza Shah (the first Pahlavi monarch and the father of Mohammad Reza Pahlavi), Iranian education was reshaped in order to create a national culture, such as Ataturk had done in Turkey.[14] A new appreciation of ancient Persia was also part of the program.[15] This appreciation of classical Persian art and literature quickly became international. Even in the late nineteenth century, officials of the Qajar Dynasty (1789–1925) supported archeological excavations in Iran, including at Persepolis.[16] In 1935, an international congress was held to commemorate the millenary of Ferdowsi (author of the Shahnameh, the Persian national epic). Forty-five delegates from eighteen different countries were in attendance. Reza Shah himself inaugurated Ferdowsi's new mausoleum, which had been constructed to resemble the tomb of Cyrus the Great.[17] Ferdowsi and Cyrus were to become important symbols for Iranian heritage and its future in the hands of the Pahlavi Dynasty. Notably absent in their public presentations, architectural style, and educational curricula were mentions of Islam and the Arab conquests that had brought it. The Pahlavi intellectual circles were, in their glorification of Persia's past, also in many cases promoting the West and the values of the Enlightenment as the future for Persia,[18] as if to crimp Islam out of history and re-envision the Arab Conquests as the Persian Dark Ages.

Also during these decades, Reza Shah instituted reforms for the de-veiling of women and in support of their education— something that had been previously denied them. In addition, the decades before the Second World War saw a turn toward European standards in general education and civil law, the emancipation of Jews and other minorities (though this seems to have been applied unevenly), the introduction of a non-Islamic calendar,[19] and efforts toward language purification (the purging of foreign words, especially Arabic, from the lexicon).[20]

Decades later, his son Mohammed Reza Shah Pahlavi continued in his father's footsteps by further supporting liberalization and equality as well as foreign investment and consumer goods.[21] In the preface to his 1961 book, *Mission for My Country*, he wrote:

> You will find this book portraying something of the impact of the West upon Iran, and my hope for a new kind of interaction between East and West. It gives a sense of the scope and pace of my country's economic development. It sets forth my three-fold idea of democracy, and the steps we have taken to help make true democracy come alive here.[22]

And in the first chapter:

> …as you go to meet a friend at Teheran's big new jet-age international airport, you pass along broad boulevards lined

The Voice of Cyrus

with modern shops, and ablaze with neon lights, where some of the women will be wearing the most daring Paris fashions, and others still be veiled.[23]

Empress Farah Pahlavi remembers Tehran in the summer of 1959 when she was an architecture student: 'That summer we danced a lot at each other's houses, listened to a huge amount of rock, and went to various cinemas.'[24]

The Shah and Shahbanu do not exaggerate Tehran's open and liberal feel. As the 1960s and 1970s wore on, the city became increasingly modern and secular, a freer place, especially for women. Magazine and pop album covers of the day show women with bare legs and cleavage—a practice curtailed immediately after the Revolution. Women across Iran emulated the short-cropped hair and miniskirt style of pop singers.[25] Author Aria Minu-Sepehr recollects:

> By the 1970s we were living in the most intense period of Westernization Iran had ever experienced, and each embrace of the new, each chic turn, posted an affront to a culture already vexed by change. In the very near past, dogs were considered eternally filthy; one lick required seven hand-washings. Pigs were vile; shrimp were vultures of the sea; drinking alcohol was a mortal sin; and women were subject to stern sanctions regarding the visibility of their hair and skin. But as far as I was concerned, dogs were our cohabitants, ham was synonymous with lunch meat, large shrimp were served with white wine, and women wore their hair long and their shorts short.[26]

But as we know, this did not last. Where it came to talk, the Shah was facile. When it came to concrete plans, he may as well have been firing an elephant gun into his own rowboat. At a press conference on December 23, 1973 (two years after

Iannis Xenakis's Persepolis

the 2,500th anniversary celebrations), the Shah announced the price of oil had quadrupled and that he alone would control the course of Iran's development, and furthermore that Iran would be the fifth most powerful country on earth within a generation. During an interview with a *Der Spiegel* journalist he was asked how this would be possible when it took Europe tens of generations to reach the current level of development. The Shah was confident he could do it in a few years. Thereafter he met with world leaders whose hands were outstretched. But he had drastically miscalculated everything and did not stop to think about the order in which things must be done. Ships arrived at port, but the ports were too small and ill-equipped to unload the cargo, so the ships sat there and had to be paid billions to wait; when they were finally unloaded, there were no warehouses to store the cargo in, so it all sat in the desert; there were no truck drivers or trucks to move the cargo anywhere. When the equipment to build factories finally arrived at their destinations, there were no engineers to direct their assembly. Instead of beginning with universities and education (perhaps fearing what the student population would think of his autocracy), he bungled the first steps toward a Great Civilization. In the end he had to order thousands of foreign specialists to manage things, and ordinary Iranians had to stand by and watch, and eventually learn to hate the foreigners. In other words, 'all of you just sit there in the shadow of the mosque and tend your sheep, because it will take a century for you to be of any use!'[27]

While the ideologues who backed the Shah saw a certain value connecting him to Cyrus, and thus imagining the Pahlavi regime as a continuation of the ancient kingship of Persia, what the Shah himself really admired was the West. He really believed Iran was some kind of 'racial' and linguistic precursor to Europe, and he really believed he would be the one to make Iran 'catch up,'[28] in the way Turkey had done in the intervening years. Cyrus was perhaps, then, not only to be thought of as the father of Persia, but also as the intellectual patriarch of Europe, via Greek philosophy. Both Herodotus and Xenophon portrayed Cyrus as a positive force in the region, the latter even referring to his compassion.[29] Plato cites Cyrus's Persia in his *Laws* as a place where the foundational qualities of liberty and free speech were permitted.[30] Alexander the Great, upon his arrival in Persia, ordered repairs to Cyrus's vandalized tomb at Pasargadae. He, like Mohammad Reza Pahlavi some 2,000 years later, was educated and saw the laws of Cyrus as a template for the future. Both these men, as rulers of Persia, found themselves in the position of having to legitimize their rule, for neither were of the lineage of Cyrus, Darius, and Xerxes. By presenting himself as the spiritual successor to Cyrus the Great, Alexander's influence spread far and wide across Eurasia and helped him secure one of the greatest empires ever known. Mohammad Reza Pahlavi, it could be argued, identified himself with Cyrus for the very same reasons.[31]

5   Shiraz, 1968–9

In 1967, the Shah's reforms were still unfolding. Along with reforms in education and literacy, women's rights under law, public health, and in agriculture and industry, the Shah also sought to open new avenues of culture for Iran. In this he knew to tread with a soft step, for his autobiography is filled with allusions to the glory and longevity of Persian culture. Although he had little interest in the arts himself, he believed that Western culture would be positive for Iranians. To this end he established the Institute for Publication and Translation of Books, which oversaw the translation of Western literary classics into Persian. In fact, he claimed to have donated all royalties from the sales of his autobiography to that initiative.[1] He also expressed an interest in Western film and music, albeit in prose so awkward one wonders how deeply he felt it:

> Although I think the American films on the whole excel in production techniques, I see superb acting and direction in some of the British, French, and Italian films…. I like our Persian music, but I must admit that the Western product shows more variety. I find waltzes and other light classical pieces agreeable and jazz diverting; but what I really care for are the great classics, especially those by Chopin, Beethoven, Schubert, Liszt, Tchaikovsky, Rimsky-Korsakov, and Borodin.[2]

Although he never articulated it in quite this way, it could be said that the Shah wanted Iran to be the center of the world, that is, the intersection of West and East, and this meant bringing Europe to Iran as much as exporting Iran elsewhere. There is an old saying about the city of Isfahan: جهان نصف اصفهان (Esfahān nesf-e jahān), which means 'Isfahan is half the world.'[3] Standing as it did at the center of the early modern commercial world, Isfahan was the place where, according to Persian poets and statesmen at the time of Shah Abbas the Great (sixteenth century), one could see each half of the world, or half of all that is the world. When we think of 'half the world' now, what comes to mind? Istanbul? Jerusalem? Had the Shah managed to see his reforms all the way through, we might today be thinking of Tehran rather than Turkey or Israel as the cultural superpower of the Middle East. Iran in the 1960s was opening up to new forms of intellectualism, but at the same time the Shah and the extremely heavy-handed secret police, SAVAK, were smashing political expressions of all kinds, unwittingly feeding the rage of both leftist opposition movements and the clerics who would together fell the state.

Included in the many and multidirectional plans for Iran's modernization was a cultural program. It was one thing to build schools and ports and pave roads, but the real test, as it were, of Westernization would be the Iranians' readiness to engage with the arts and literature of the world. At that time, much of Iranian cultural life and its public spaces, including cinema, theaters, and concert halls, fell under the direction of the Ministry of Information and the Ministry of Art and Culture.[4] The Shiraz-Persepolis Festival of Art was the initiative of Empress Farah Pahlavi. The Shahbanu, a student of architecture in Paris prior to her engagement to the Shah, saw the prospering of Iranian arts and their engagement with the international arts scene as supportive of the turn toward participatory democracy. In consultation with her cousin Reza Ghotbi, who was also the director of National Iranian Television

(NITV), the Shahbanu hosted an annual international arts festival in Iran, featuring both traditional and modern arts.[5]

The Shiraz Festival debuted in 1967 under the auspices of the Empress Farah, who inaugurated each year's events, and Sharazad Ghotbi, a violinist (and wife of Reza Ghotbi), who was appointed musical director. The progressive programming year to year was designed to present an evolving world to Iranian audiences, while the artist selections largely reflected the empress's tastes in art, which leaned heavily into the contemporary.[6] Its other purpose was 'to be an occasion for Iranian artists to expand their horizons and for non-Iranian visitors to get acquainted with the cultural heritage of Iran.'[7]

During the planning stages in the mid-1960s, it was decided that in order to jumpstart the cultural life of the Iranian provinces the festival would not be held in Tehran. Kashan and Isfahan were briefly considered as venues, but they lacked proper infrastructure for hundreds of festivalgoers. In the end, Shiraz was chosen not only because it was better equipped to host hundreds of people in its university dormitories, but also because of its weather, wine, and hospitable people, and proximity to Persepolis—'a living museum of Iranian architecture through which the eternal spirit of the nation was revealed.'[8] And the organizers thought the ruins would work perfectly as a theater. In addition, Shiraz is Iran's city of poets and painters. Both Saadi (1213–91) and Hafez (1324–89) are buried there,[9] and the latter poet's tomb has long served as a concert venue.

The weeklong festival was held in eleven editions, from 1967 to 1977. Over the years it featured a surprisingly forward-looking and un-commercial musical cast: a Balinese gamelan ensemble, the Senegalese National Ballet, the Max Roach Quintet, Ustad Vilayat Khan, Yehudi Menuhin, Merce

Cunningham, John Cage, David Tudor, Gordon Mumma, Dariush Dolat-Shahi, performances of the Persian passion play *Ta'zieh* (which portrays the founding of Shi'a Islam), Karlheinz Stockhausen, and, of course, Iannis Xenakis.[10] In 1972, American theater director Robert Wilson staged *Ka Mountain*, a 168-hour play, involving some 700 people, over the course of a week in the landscape of the Haft Tan Mountains on the outskirts of Shiraz, spreading into the city itself.[11] Thus, no one spectator could ever witness the entire play. In 1975, the Nō Theater of Japan performed, reportedly for the first time ever outside Japan. Even the leftist Bread and Puppet Theater was invited, and, in 1970, they daringly staged an anti-Shah performance, and this was tolerated.[12]

Aside from this international commitment, the Shiraz Festival also served as patron to Iranian classical music. Numerous Iranian musicians, many unknown even inside the country, were featured alongside the recognizable names in Euro-American avant-gardism and classicism. The organizers were apparently quite happy about this contrast. Farrokh Ghaffari, a member of the festival committee, had deployed volunteers to search the farthest corners of the country for traditional Iranian artists of all kinds. They found an unanticipated treasure trove of poets, storytellers, marionette troupes, theater groups, and traditional bands, all with local styles and bearing centuries-old traditions. Empress Farah referred to it as 'an embarrassment of riches.'[13]

The audience for the festivals apparently took to the more avant-garde of the proceedings. Gordon Mumma recollects the festivalgoers in Shiraz as more serious and interested than those in New York and Europe: 'There were none of the aggressive arguments about "that isn't music" stuff that we often encountered elsewhere.'[14] Likewise, when the Iranian musicians played, '[s]eats, carpets, and cushions were laid out in the [gardens of Hafez's Tomb], and as night fell, little candles were lit on each side of the path. So many came to listen that people would even be sitting out in the street.'[15] At other times, things were less tranquil. University students periodically confronted the artists, asking them whether they were aware that by taking part in the festival they were supporting a dictatorship. To one such question, Polish playwright Jerzy Grotowski allegedly replied, 'If you really believed what you say you'd be up there in the mountains with a machine gun, rather than talking calmly with me here.'[16]

How did Xenakis appear on the radar of the festival organizers? There is more than one possibility. An obvious link between Paris and Shiraz would be French music critic Claude Samuel, who was music programmer for the Royan Festival, which premiered Xenakis's *Terretektorh* in 1966 and *Nuits* in 1968,[17] as well as an advisor to the Shiraz committee,[18] which also elected to feature the same piece in its 1968 program. However, in an interview with Enzo Restagno, Xenakis explains that it was in fact Mehdi Boushehri, the Shah's brother-in-law (married to his twin sister Ashraf) and head of the Paris film company Les Films de l'Astrophore,[19] who enlisted him. According to Xenakis, Boushehri had 'followed the Royan Festival from the very beginning and had the idea of founding a festival in his own country.'[20] Boushehri himself did not found the Shiraz Festival, but it is quite possible that he attended *Nuits* at Royan in 1968 and recommended it to the festival organizers.

Originally commissioned by the Gulbenkian Foundation, *Nuits* is an a cappella vocal work made up of syllables from Mycenæan, Sumerian, and Persian texts.[21] Removed from their context, and thus from meaning, these phonemes become shards of pure expression for the human voice. *Nuits* is remarkable among Xenakis's works in that it is the first time Xenakis makes an overt political gesture, in dedicating the score

> to you, unknown political prisoners—Narcisso Julian (since 1946), Costas Philinis (since 1947), Eli Erythriadou (since 1950), Joachim Amaro (since 1952). And for you, the thousands of the forgotten whose very names are lost.[22]

The year was 1968 and Xenakis was well aware of the struggles against nationalism and dictators around Europe. The four political prisoners named in the preface to the score of *Nuits* are very obscure indeed, but he meant them to be examples of the unremembered thousands swallowed by the struggle against Franco's Spain and Salazar's Portugal, as well as the turmoil in postwar Greece. The year 1968 was a memorable one in France. Its nationwide strikes, occupations, and anti-de Gaulle protests are the stuff of legend among leftists, Marxists, and all those who foresaw the deleterious effects of rising consumerism in Europe. If Xenakis believed in the struggle against authoritarian regimes, why would he submit his artistic support to the Shah's regime? Why not add to his dedication the names of the Iranian political prisoners murdered by SAVAK?

This question has been asked many times. Did he feel a sense of conflict or compromise in rubbing elbows with the Shah, or, like many others in those days, however naïvely, did he believe the Shah's progressive attitude was the best hope for Iran? Xenakis would make his views on the Shah's regime—and democracy itself—clear enough in an open letter to *Le Monde* four months after the premiere of *Persepolis* (see **Chapter 8**).

As alluded to in this letter, by reading the dedication of *Nuits* aloud at the 1968 festival[23] he was indeed commenting on the fate of political prisoners in Iran. A risk, but a calculated risk. And he was invited back the next year.

With the premiere of *Persephassa*[24] at the 1969 Shiraz Festival, Xenakis experienced the acoustic dynamics of Persepolis for the first time. No surviving journals record his first impressions of the ruined ancient city, its stone columns, its great stairway, its stables and passageways, but as an architect he must have marveled at it all and thought carefully about its properties as a theater (**Figure 6**). *Persephassa*, a percussion work, requires its six players to position themselves in a hexagonal formation surrounding the audience. At the Persepolis site, and with an audience of several hundred, this must have meant they were quite far apart from one another. The synchronized percussion layers build to a final passage of 360 beats per minute, each player coming in at a different tempo, thus creating a complex counterpoint.[25] It must have been an astonishing experience to be consumed by this thirty-minute sound cloud. And it is easy to imagine the audience present reflecting on the ritual

Figure 6 *Persepolis, Palace of Darius.*

activity that took place 2,000 years before on the ground where they stood. It is also easy to imagine Xenakis standing among the ruins and devising an even more spectacular multimedia show, which would become the Polytope de Persépolis two years later.

In 1967, the year before presenting *Nuits* to the crowds at Shiraz, Xenakis realized his first polytope[26] at Montréal's French Pavilion (now the Casino de Montréal). This media installation, presented in connection with Expo 67, featured an integrated show of sculpture, light, and sound, designed by Xenakis. No doubt encouraged by his experience with the Philips Pavilion and *Le poème électronique*, his interest in a multimedia spectacle seems to have reached deeper. The 1960s were the first decade of space travel. Artists and authors everywhere were aware of the potential of space technology to further the human destiny. Xenakis himself dreamed of designing a *ville cosmique*—a cosmic city above the clouds that would put human beings

> in contact with the vast spaces of the sky and the stars: the planetary and cosmic era has begun, and the [concept of the] city will have to be turned towards the cosmos and its human colonies, instead of remaining in a state of crawling.[27]

Like the Philips Pavilion, the *ville cosmique* would be a 5,000-meter-tall hyperbolic shell, 50 meters thick, containing homes, public spaces, workplaces, and so on, for 5 million people.[28] The fascination with human life in the three dimensions of human space led to experiments in three-dimensional art. Just as *Metastaseis* was an experiment in freeing music from stasis and linearity, Xenakis's polytopes were an effort to free art from two dimensions. They were to be a 'total spectacle, a festival for all five senses,'[29] an 'attempt to develop a new form of art with light and sound.'[30]

Xenakis also claimed he 'was attracted by the idea of repeating on a lower level what Nature carries out on a grand scale. The notion of Nature covers not only the earth but also the universe.' He was fascinated by the idea that the lights on earth that we see from space didn't exist a century ago, and if we extrapolate in terms of cultural development, the 'possibilities of mankind will multiply and all that novelty will also enrich art.'[31]

Visitors to the Polytope de Montréal entered the central plaza of the pavilion and suddenly, once per hour, beheld a storm of pointillistic light, as cast through 1,200 photosensitive cells and filtered through holes in a perforated tape. Xenakis calculated by hand the 19,000 successive events of the light show, which he himself described as 'a kind of transparent sculpture.'[32] This was accompanied by a soundtrack of slow-paced glissandi, as played by four eleven-person orchestras situated at the four cardinal points of the concert hall. The tape recording of this performance was broadcast from speakers installed among the cables and lights. The six-minute Polytope de Montréal looped continuously and was designed to be heard in infinite ways from different positions on the multiple levels of the French Pavilion.[33]

With the success of the Polytope de Montréal, Xenakis began to receive further commissions for audiovisual work, both at future Expos and independent art-and-technology events. With this reputation he would also be invited to return to Iran in 1971 to take part in the Fifth Annual Shiraz Arts Festival, which took place the same year as the Shah's 2,500th anniversary celebration. The two events are best thought of as separate, even if Xenakis's contribution was meant to be a commemoration of Persian history. But there was also an unintentional irony in the inclusion of Xenakis, a Greek—like Alexander the Great, who destroyed Persepolis in 330 BCE. Now a second Greek was coming, armed with fire, and a soundtrack of strongly European avant-garde music. Such ironies were not lost on those who claim the Shiraz Festival, and the 2,500th anniversary celebrations 'paved the way for the Islamic reaction and was therefore one of the causes of the overthrow of the monarchy.'[34]

6 Paris, 1971

In late 1970 or early 1971, Xenakis received an official invitation from the organizers of the Shiraz Festival to participate a third time. This year's events would be different than before, as they would be held on the same year as the 2,500th anniversary celebration of the founding of the Persian Empire. Accordingly, the organizers asked Xenakis to develop a *son et lumière* for premiere at the opening of the 1971 Shiraz Festival on the night of August 26, at the Persepolis archeological site. Having premiered *Persephassa* at the site in 1969, Xenakis was familiar with its landscape, architecture, and acoustic dynamics. This time he would expand the scope of the Polytope de Persépolis out from the Apadana and Tachara to include the nearby hillsides and the Naqsh-e Rostam, the necropolis where the lineages of Darius the Great are buried.[1]

Although there are no extant journals detailing his thoughts on how he hoped the raw sounds and structure of the eight tracks of *Persepolis* would interact with the physical site in the desert, it is possible to reconstruct his creative process and mixing of the sounds in the studio, as well as something of the audio experience at Persepolis. *Persepolis* was the most technically complex sound-assembly process Xenakis had undertaken. He began by collecting found sounds, some (but not all) of which he identifies in the sketch plan for the work. These include ceramic wind chimes, a Japanese gong, wind, an airplane, timpani rolls, clarinets, strings, and the sounds of cardboard being folded. The rest are difficult to identify.[2] In the

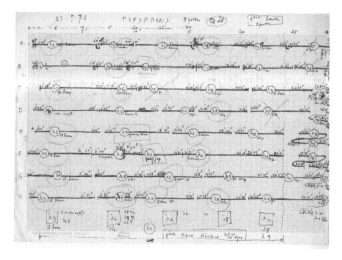

Figure 7 Persepolis *'score.'*

final product, the elements have no independent life, blending into the whole of this *musique concrète* work. The score for this piece was almost as painstakingly assembled as the work itself (**Figure 7**). On graph paper, Xenakis pasted carefully measured paper strips representing the sequence of the *objets sonores*, which he called 'lambda elements.' The character of each element (e.g., 'carton,' 'jet') and its position in the structure of the work are noted on the paper. While each always lasted the same length of time, he avoided repetitions by varying the attack point or by using different sections of the same material.[3]

Xenakis made a second, even more elaborate score for use in performance. For this one he adhered strips of colored paper to represent the groups of lambda elements arranged in sequence to form the layers of the sound mass that is *Persepolis*.[4] Can this graphic illustration of the work really be called a score, though? It does not, after all, tell us anything about the sensibilities of the sound material, like a standard score with notation does. If the score of Mahler's *Symphony No. 2* is a linguistic rendering of the music, by which future conductors and musicians can get very close to how Mahler himself conducted it, the score for *Persepolis* is more like a recipe. You still have to learn the physical properties of the sound elements in order to recreate—or for that matter, remix and remaster—the work.

Today, the process of sequencing and layering blocks of concrete sound to form a sound mass, and even broadcasting them live via multiple speakers, is an everyday occurrence. It can be done on a laptop. In 1971, no one had done anything quite this way in the studio before. Stockhausen, Penderecki, Ferrari, Oliveros, and the other innovators of the day were working with similar sonic density, but with orchestras and various other studio techniques. Xenakis was layering eight tracks of sound objects that were themselves morphing and changing into a representation of the history of Iran, and all this in turn was keyed to the choreography of the overall event.

In the program notes booklet that was distributed at the event, Xenakis described *Persepolis* in characteristically physical terms:

> This music corresponds to a rock tablet on which hieroglyphic or cuneiform messages are engraved in a compact hermetic way; delivering their secrets only to those who want and know how to read them. The history of Iran, a fragment of the world's history, is thus elliptically and abstractly represented by means of clashes, explosions, continuities and underground currents of sound.[5]

The first step in constructing the master tapes was to record two mono tape reels with each lambda element placed one after another in sequence.[6] Since the master tapes were to contain eight tracks, he arranged the sound elements in real-time sequence on two sets of eight reels—a total of sixteen mono reels, two for each track of the master tapes—which he mixed at Studio Acousti,[7] 54, rue de Seine, near the Boulevard Saint Germain in Paris. (The studio is no longer in operation, and its founder, Alain Cluzeau, could not be reached for comment.)

Studio Acousti's roster throughout the decades has been quite eclectic. The Ron Jefferson Choir, the Nathan Davis Quartet, Flamenco guitarist Claude Puyalte, Jacques Prévert (for a children's record), and the folk group Malicorne all recorded at Acousti. Xenakis may have chosen this studio over others in Paris for its capacity to mix sixteen tracks—something not every studio would have been willing or able to do in 1971. And by that time Pierre Schaeffer's Studio d'Essai was no longer an option. According to the 1971 Studio Acousti price sheet found among Xenakis's personal effects, the studio possessed a 16-track Ampex recorder and a 24-channel AMS Neve console for mixing and mastering.[8]

These 8-track audio reels used for the Polytope de Persépolis were the same that Xenakis would master for release as an LP record the following year by Philips. The original edition of this record (Philips 6521 045) formed part of the label's Prospective 21e Siècle series, as curated by François Bayle and Pierre Henry. As part of this series, *Persepolis* found a home among the leading French *musique concrète* and electronic artists of the day, including Bernard Parmegiani, Luc Ferrari, Pierre Schaeffer, and Ivo Malec, not to mention Bayle and Henry themselves.

Once the two *Persepolis* reels were mixed, Xenakis could focus on the details of the *son et lumière*. It is one thing to record an 8-track album in a Paris studio. It is another thing to broadcast it in a 2,500-year-old ruin made of limestone blocks, mud bricks, and cedar wood beams and columns, and to synchronize it with lasers and a procession of lights some distance away. Even in Tehran it would have been difficult to find the electronics equipment needed for on-the-spot repairs, unexpected adjustments to position, diffusion, and so on, much less 60 km from Shiraz in Iran's Fars Province. Xenakis's final schematic for the audio outlines the setup in the six contiguous listening areas in the ruin. In each such 'room' either eight or sixteen speakers would be distributed, clockwise or counterclockwise. Each set of eight speakers broadcast one track (which Xenakis designated A-H) of the 8-track recording of *Persepolis* to a standing audience.[9]

Xenakis had initially hoped to outfit the ruin with 800 speakers in a grid pattern, as well as employ a helicopter as part of the lighting. Perhaps having been told it would be difficult enough to import sound equipment to Iran, he curtailed these plans, though he did succeed in obtaining and using two laser lights.[10] In the end he chose, or was forced, to scale the lights show to a much more modest scale, that of torches, car headlamps, and gasoline fires on the hillside over Persepolis.

Xenakis conducted the elements of the *son et lumière* from the site. Of the many challenging tasks was the coordination of audio reels. In 1971, a standard reel contained no more than forty minutes of tape; yet, *Persepolis* was nearly an hour in length. In order to broadcast the work without interruption, he set up two 8-track tape machines side by side and crossfaded between the two reels.[11] In addition, because of the historic importance of Persepolis, no renovations or compromises to the fabric of the site could be made. Therefore, the fifty-nine speakers, ninety-two spotlights, and two lasers had to be integrated into the space without so much as a bolt or a nail (see **Chapter 7**).

The silver-foil Héliophore cover of the original LPs (as designed by Jacques Hardelin of the Office Central de l'Imagerie for Philips)[12] and all subsequent reissues feature an epigraph, in French and English: *Nous portons la lumière de la terre/We bear the light of the earth*. This phrase would form part of the culmination of the Polytope de Persépolis in 1971. Xenakis offers no further explanation of its meaning. He did, however, explain the motivations behind *Persepolis* in a 1971 interview with an Iranian journalist: 'The children represent "the hope of humanity and the people of Iran." And the lights and fire represents [sic] truth and the God of the ancient Persians— Ahura Mazda.'[13] He later expanded on the symbolism in a letter to *Le Monde*: 'It is a tribute to Iran's past and her great Zoroastrian and Manichean revolutionaries, and their ramifications to the Paulicians, Bogomiles and Cathars of Byzantium, Italy, Germany and France.'[14] Among the oddly assorted historical communities he lists, Zoroastrianism would seem to be the key to understanding the meaning of this beguiling phrase.

The Zoroastrian 'revolutionary' Xenakis refers to here is Zoroaster himself. This Greek version of the prophet's name has even been translated as meaning 'living star' (*zoro*, ζωρός = living, *aster*, ἄστρον = star), the bringer of light to earth.[15] The myth of Zoroaster's life depicts him as having undergone a series of angelic visions, through which he was instructed to reveal divine Truth to people on earth, in order that good would triumph over evil.[16] If Xenakis saw this as a revolutionary act, perhaps it is because he identified with imprisonment for one's beliefs, and with the nearly miraculous conditions of freedom and the effort to create something better out of life. Zoroaster himself was imprisoned for the threat his beliefs posed to the learned men of the court. He was released only because, when the king's best horse fell ill, only Zoroaster could cure it—which he agreed to do only if the court converted to his religion and allow him to go forth and crusade for the faith.[17] Xenakis described himself as

> a wandering man, an 'alien citizen' of every country (in art as well) and my hardened conscience—nourished either by the flames of the Greek resistance (which was betrayed from its conception and over the years by the Soviets, the Allies and the Greeks themselves) or by the desperate efforts of my music—alone, may guide me towards light or towards death.[18]

What Zoroaster brought to the adherents of his religion was a prediction that good could overcome evil in the world, under the guidance of a single supreme being, Ahura Mazda.[19] The pervading presence of fire in all Zoroastrian (and early Vedic Hindu) scripture must ultimately rest with the expedience of heat and light for the desert nomads who ritualized it. But according to Zoroastrian cosmology, ritual fire is the channel through which the world of man and the world of Ahura Mazda are connected—the offerings of man are taken up and the wisdom of God is brought back down.[20] According to the *Avesta*, the final judgment will also be rendered by fire (in this case a blade forged from it): 'And this I will announce by means of Thy flaming fire; yea, I will declare it for the bestowal of that sword of justice which is forged from steel, and wrought for both the worlds. And for the wounding of the wicked (with its blade) may'st Thou, O Ahura Mazda! bless and prosper Thine (avenging) saint!'[21]

The Manichean revolutionary Xenakis refers to could be the prophet Mani himself (who was born into the Zoroastrian-dominated Parthian Empire of Persia), or perhaps the 'First Man' of Manichean mythology, who battled the forces of darkness and lost. But in being consumed by darkness, the darkness absorbed the light of his soul into itself, and thus the act was a self-sacrifice.[22]

The battle of light and darkness at the heart of Zoroastrian and Manichean cosmology has a parallel in the Prometheus story, which Xenakis, a Greek educated in Greece, would surely have known well. The trickster Prometheus creates humans from clay and gives them fire. Zeus, angered when the humans are given a better portion of sacrificial meat than he, takes the fire away so that humans must forever eat uncooked meat in darkness and cold. Seeing the injustice in this, Prometheus ventures to Mount Olympus and steals back the fire in a hollow fennel-stalk and gives it to the humans, for which both they and Prometheus are punished in chains.[23]

The bearers of light on earth in the pageantry of the Polytope de Persépolis were not heroic revolutionaries in the literary tradition, but rather anonymous torch-bearing schoolchildren from Shiraz. Maybe Xenakis appreciated the potential of their obscurity in the same way he lauded the 'unknown political prisoners,' Narcisso Julian, Costas Philinis, Eli Erythriadou, and Joachim Amaro in the dedication of *Nuits*. The schoolchildren were, after all, as one journalist put it, 'the people of Iran, their future,' and thus 'and a general hope for humanity.'[24] One wonders how many of them went on to participate in the revolution that was to come. One wonders also whether Xenakis, in his elevation of Zoroastrian and Manichean cosmology, was aware of the Zoroastrian revivalist (and consequently anti-Arab, anti-Islam) strains among contemporary nationalists.[25] Or perhaps, more generally, he was satisfied with the potential of his own light and sound work to combat the forces of darkness he saw lurking in plain sight:

For me, the worst and most shameful injustice is the torture and execution (either secretly or overtly) of men and women, even if they are 'terrorists.' This is why I have always been involved, and will continue to be, in protests and actions against dynasties and tyrants, be they military, heads of state, presidents, shahs, or kings. It is in my nature.[26]

7   Persepolis, 1971

Xenakis arrived in Iran in August 1971, ahead of the opening of the Fifth Annual Shiraz Festival. The first day mentioned in his notes is 'Saturday 4:00 p.m. first rehearsal.'[1] This likely was Saturday, August 21, five days before the premiere on Thursday, August 26. But he may have been on-site before this date to install the multi-channel speaker system inside the Persepolis ruin.[2] Xenakis doesn't describe how he mounted the speakers, but since he couldn't drill holes into the stone, mudbrick, and wood fabrics of the Great Palace of Xerxes, it appears he mounted them on stands in listening areas.[3] It is also not clear who helped Xenakis with the setup. He lists only three names as his technical staff: Pakravan, Azmi, and Esraili.[4] Presumably they were local craftsmen or French-speaking technicians who assisted him with the complex arrangements of sound, lighting, and the corralling of 130 Shiraz schoolchildren. Also on hand was a small French film crew headed by Pierre Andrégui, whose documentary film about the event, *Xenakis: Persepolis* (1971), contains the only officially released footage of the premiere.[5]

At 4:00 p.m. on August 26, the festival opened with a performance of *Alice in Wonderland* by André Gregory's theater company, The Manhattan Project.[6] Then, four hours later, at 8:00 p.m., the Polytope de Persépolis would begin, with Her Imperial Majesty the Shahbanu of Iran in attendance.[7]

It was already dark when the audience arrived at the Persepolis ruin and entered the courtyard of the Great Palace

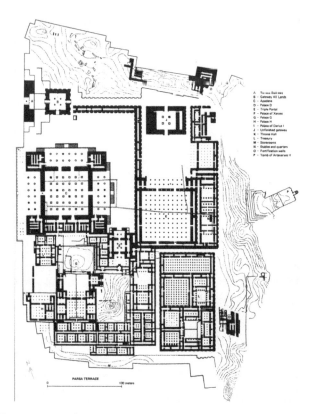

A - Terrace Stairway
B - Gateway All Lands
C - Apadana
D - Palace D
E - Triple Portal
F - Palace of Xerxes
G - Palace G
H - Palace H
I - Palace of Darius I
J - Unfinished gateway
K - Throne Hall
L - Treasury
M - Storerooms
N - Stables and quarters
O - Fortification walls
P - Tomb of Artaxerxes II

PARSA TERRACE

0   100 meters

Figure 8 *Map of the Persepolis ruin.*

of Xerxes (**Figure 8**). For a time, they milled around in the six contiguous listening areas in near darkness, waiting for something to come from the speakers along the walls. Xenakis himself was stationed somewhere inside the ruin, at a vantage point from which he could see the hills and hear the dynamics of the fifty-nine multi-channel speakers (**Figure 9**). From there he directed the spectacle with a walkie-talkie.[8] At the appointed hour, the speakers began emitting Xenakis's 1957 *musique concrète* piece *Diamorphoses* (see **Chapter 3**) as a prelude to the main event.[9] After this seven-minute opener, there was a silence for a time as Xenakis spooled the first reel of *Persepolis*. Then, with the first churning tone, the nearly one-hour *son et lumière* touches off and immediately the hillsides above the ruin are engulfed in light. Two gigantic gasoline bonfires are ignited at the Naqsh-e Rostam necropolis, where the lineages of Darius and Artaxerxes are buried. Added to the fires are light from battery-powered car headlamps, pointed skyward, and from red laser beams sweeping across the ruins.[10]

The audience that night included foreign dignitaries, journalists, students, and other participants in the festival. Few would have been prepared for the unfolding sound textures coming at them through the loudspeakers. To them the elliptical motion of textures must have sounded like rubbed glass, treated air, and the scraping together of large steel sheets, the sound wrapping itself around the rooms. In the first minute alone, the sounds expand and contract, rise and fall, burrowing up like the elements in times of geologic turmoil, from unimaginable depths, oxidizing and crystallizing on the surface into forms that in turn decay and return to the earth, like civilizations. As Xenakis wrote, 'Symbol of history's noise; unassailable rocks facing the assault of the waves of civilization … The history of Iran, fragment of the world's history, is thus elliptically and abstractly represented by means of clashes, explosions, continuities and underground currents of sound.'[11] The more attuned audience members would have heard these sonic forces—deep grinding and higher-pitched glistening—seemingly at odds acoustically, yet not in conflict, forming a biotic whole. They would also have realized that the work to which they were listening had no harmonic structure, no breaks, and no sections.

Soon after the soundtrack begins, several groups of Shiraz schoolboys, about 130 in all, have gathered with torches at

Figure 9 *Iannis Xenakis at the control board, Persepolis, August 1971.*

the base of the hillside. In view of the listening audience, they climb to the summit of the hill, in the direction of the fires, and stand, forming an outline of light between the crest and the sky. During the performance, a dust storm blows in from the desert,[12] unexpectedly adding a dream-haze to the light and sound. After a time, the children descend, making constellation-like lines with their torches.[13] On the hillside, in the space between the ancient tombs, the children spread out in formation to spell, in Persian, *We Bear the Light of the Earth* with the light from their torches (**Figure 10**). The torchbearers then run toward the audience and disappear among the Apadana (the Palace of 1000 Columns). With that, the fifty-nine loudspeakers in the Persepolis ruin go silent, for one hour has passed.[14]

Xenakis's notes (as jotted down by his wife Françoise) give some indication of what he and his small crew were up to behind the scenes: 'All 130 hidden behind the hillock (pyramid) … Do the bonfire here … Walkie-talkie … Call Philips … White paint? … Laser … Unlit table … On the summit (projectors plus lasers) … The seventh group … Three meters … Never stop, never group together … A stop watch for the first.'[15]

It was essential for Xenakis that the torchbearers be schoolchildren, not adults. As he explained in the program booklet for the event: 'Childhood's awakening must be maintained because it represents active knowledge, perpetual questioning that forges the becoming of man…. groups of children will bear torches along the mountain and the Apadana. Laser beams, focused on the past's holes [tombs] will

Figure 10 *Torch-bearing schoolchildren from Shiraz spell out* We Bear the Light of the Earth *in Persian during the Persepolis Polytope, August 26, 1971.*

fuse with the light-string of children, the peoples' future has been and will-be linked by light.'[16]

Xenakis expounded further on the meaning behind the lights and choreography in the festival program booklet:

> To invent light trajectories, to create signs, destinies on stone: mountains, ruins, of ourselves, through sound, through fire, through light. Lights, sempiternal lights…. 'Persepolis' is neither a theatrical spectacle, nor a ballet, nor a happening. It is visual symbolism, parallel to and dominated by sound. The sound, the music, must absolutely prevail. … The listener must pay for his penetration into the knowledge of the signs with great effort, pain and the suffering of his own birth.[17]

It is true that the Shah and his consort had in mind a modern, European-leaning Iran. By the 1970s, this push for techno-modernity and secular governance was tinged with revivalist and monarchical rhetoric (via Cyrus) and allusions to ancient Iran.[18] Even so, it is difficult to say with certainty that the inclusion of Modernist musicians, playwrights, filmmakers, and so on in the Shiraz Arts Festival lineup was part of this program. The Shiraz Festival rosters reflected the tastes of the Shahbanu and her programming circle. The Shah himself probably had no idea who Iannis Xenakis was or what his music sounded like. According to one researcher he was not even present the night of August 26 for the premiere of *Persepolis*, even if the empress certainly was.[19] This takes away nothing from the theories that Xenakis, Stockhausen, and the rest of the modern or avant-garde artisans at the Shiraz Festivals were contributing to what one Iranian critic termed *gharbzadegi*, or occidentosis (see **Chapter 8**). Xenakis's *Persepolis* was about as traditional as possible in its theme, with appreciations of Zoroaster, Mani, Persia, and the influence of these on world history (this deeper layer was lost on the clerics and critics who were apparently more concerned with Islam than with tradition), but the music itself could not have emanated, in 1971, from anywhere but Europe. Not only was it devoid of harmonies, melodies, and all other features of classical music, it was *hermetic*. It had to be deciphered, and furthermore, to comprehend the music was to pay a price: the pain and agony of consciousness.

It wasn't just religious conservatives who felt a sense of *gharbzadegi*. Even the Iranian composer Alireza Mashayekhi (who has worked with Western instrumentation, including atonal compositions and works for tape) lamented the festivals: 'Historically, in a country that has no tradition in Classical music and no acquaintance with contemporary music, the festival had the appearance of an invasion…. The presence of composers like Mr. Stockhausen and the late Mr. Xenakis was a miserable example of opportunism.'[20]

In a certain way, the criticisms of the festivals as too modernist, too European, too lavish, too expensive were more strongly concerned with money than with aesthetics. The Persian-language volumes of SAVAK documents about the Shiraz Festivals mention Stockhausen in unflattering terms (Xenakis is not mentioned at all), indicating they thought his work was simply stupid, not dangerous, and why spend money on such nonsense. The opinion of the Shia clerics was very similar.[21] But the October celebrations were another matter altogether. Indeed, much of the ire over the 2,500th anniversary rose to a boil over events for which Xenakis was not even present.

* * *

On Tuesday October 12, 1971, the celebrations of the 2,500th anniversary of the Persian Empire continued at Pasargadae with a ceremony in honor of Cyrus the Great (see **Chapter 4**). At 11:00 a.m., with the audience of ministers, journalists, foreign and Iranian academics, army brass, and religious leaders already seated, the Shah and Shahbanu arrived by helicopter. The Shah emerged at 11:30 from the royal tent to the sound of the national anthem, followed by a 101-gun salute. Then the imperial family joined him in the open area before Cyrus's tomb and he stepped forward to place a wreath below the steps. He stood in silence for one minute, and at 11:36 a.m. began his oration honoring the ancient king—the first modernizer, the first champion of religious freedoms, the great peacemaker—for his moral and spiritual gifts to the world.[22]

Following this emotionally charged forty-five-minute ceremony, the airplanes of the heads of state and other honored guests began to arrive at Shiraz Airport. There they were greeted by the Shah's brothers and escorted in a fleet of 250 Mercedes-Benz 600 limousines[23] to Persepolis, where they were greeted by the Shah and Shahbanu themselves. To each guest, the Shah said, 'In the name of the empress and myself, I welcome you to Iran on the occasion of the twenty-fifth-hundred anniversary of our monarchy.' The head of state was then invited to stand with the Shah on a podium and listen to his or her national anthem played by the Imperial Guard band.[24] Among the 162 dignitaries present for the celebrations were Vice President Spiro Agnew, Prince Philip and Princess Anne, Nikolai Podgorny (Chairman of the Presidium of the Supreme Soviet of the USSR), President V. V. Giri of India, Emperor Haile Selassie of Ethiopia, Crown Prince Carl Gustaf of Sweden, Sultan Qaboos bin Said al Said of Oman, King Constantine II and Queen Anne-Marie of Greece, Aga Khan IV and Begum Om Habibeh Aga Khan, First Lady Imelda Marcos of the Philippines, and President Nicolae and First Lady Elena Ceauşescu of Romania.[25]

The guests were served an informal lunch and dinner and were offered the opportunity to see local sites such as Naqsh-e Rostam, the Aryamehr Farm, the Darius Dam, or simply to play mini-golf. Some heads of state took the opportunity to go further afield in Iran, even as far as Mashhad, Bandar Pahlavi, and Rāmsar.[26] The VIP guests were lodged in private apartments within the massive tent city built near Persepolis. The tent city itself was designed and manufactured by a Paris-based interior design firm called Maison Jansen. Each tent was uniquely designed, but all 'consisted of a sitting room, two bedrooms, two bathrooms and a service room' and were arranged in spoke pattern of five lanes, at the center of which was a fountain.[27] Each lane was named for a continent. The Shah's own enormous tent and the banquet hall sat adjacent to the rest.[28] The guest suites themselves were decorated with Persian carpets, and each head of state found his likeness on a souvenir silk carpet with the Persepolis site in the background. The bathrooms were stocked with French toiletries such as Guerlain shaving kits for men and Joy Eau de Cologne for women. Linens and towels were provided by Porthault Jours de Paris. Ahead of the event, the event planners circulated a questionnaire concerning dietary requirements, breakfast food choices, beverage brands, and types of cigars and cigarettes to be made available. Aside from these small gestures of elegance, the tents were in no way extravagantly decorated, and reports of marble bathtubs, for example, appear to be media exaggerations.[29]

Elsewhere in the tent city, fully equipped hair salons were set up and renowned hairdressers were flown in to coif the hair of the first ladies and princesses for the main event.[30] Catering was handled by Maxim's of Paris, which at the time boasted a three-star rank in the Michelin guide.[31] Waiters and sommeliers were also imported from Europe.[32] The decision to use a French caterer instead of serving traditional Persian cuisine, according to the organizers, was a matter of capability. No Iranian caterer or restaurant could manage a banquet of 600 people over the course of several days. On the one hand, it was a difficult decision, for the organizers knew the criticisms would come—and they did come, from all quarters. Why, after 2,500 years of glorious civilization, Foreign Minister Ardeshir Zahedi asked rhetorically, can we not serve the guests 'Persian dishes like *kabab kubideh* or even *ab-gusht*?'[33] (On the second night, October 15th, guests were, in fact, served a buffet of Iranian dishes.)[34] At a press conference where journalists had asked the Shah to respond to questions about the enormous cost of the event, he reacted, 'Why are we reproached for serving dinner to 50 heads of state? What am I supposed to do, give them bread and radishes?'[35] The press was merciless about the food. Before the event had even begun, a *Daily Mail* article fulminated, 'There'll be 18 kinds of cheeses. The bill for the saucisson alone is reckoned to be £500. And somebody has ordered 50 kippers. Who's the kipper maniac on the list?'[36]

Guests at the October 14 evening banquet enjoyed a six-course dinner over five hours. While catered and delivered by Maxim's, the banquet was designed by the renowned Max Blouet,[37] longtime manager of the George V in Paris. The Limoges porcelain dinnerware was designed by D. Porthault.[38] On it was served saddles of lamb,[39] roast imperial peacocks, quail's eggs stuffed with Iranian caviar (the only Iranian element in the meal), mousse of crawfish tails, and champagne sorbet.[40] The wine and champagne menu featured Chateau

Lafite (1945), Blanc de Blancs, Moët Chandon (1911), and Dom Perignon Rosé (1959).[41]

When the banquet had concluded, the guests were guided out to the Persepolis site, down the same dusty trail the Shiraz Festival attendees had walked a few weeks before. There is film footage of this caravan of dignitaries making their way in the night. Leading the caravan is Empress Farah, in her gown and bejeweled crown, escorted by Haile Selassie I of Ethiopia. The crowd passes by the ancient Persian bas-reliefs, professionally daylit by the same company that managed lighting at the Palace of Versailles.[42] As the film footage ends, the crowd is seated in what looks like metal stadium bleachers, awaiting the evening's event. The desert is cold at night, so the guests were given blankets to wrap themselves in (and possibly also some brandy and whiskey in small bottles).[43]

The event that night was another a *son et lumière* and multimedia pageant with a narration of Achaemenid Persian history at Persepolis—this time without Xenakis's involvement at all. Instead, the soundtrack was provided by Armenian-Iranian composer Loris Tjeknavorian, whose neoclassical piece, also entitled *Persepolis*, was played throughout the pageant.[44] The narration began with the voice of Artaxerxes II recounting the construction of Persepolis, the 1,000 clay tablets in the Persepolis library, the institution of a twelve-hour clock, the Achaemenid postal service, and so on,[45] as actors dressed in Achaemenid costumes performed the rites of the ancient kings while lights flashed Zoroastrian patterns on the walls.[46] Ahura Mazda and Cyrus also made theatrical appearances.[47] As the pageantry ended, the lights were supposed to come back on, reilluminating Persepolis. But they didn't. Something was wrong. Three or four minutes went by. Some guests believed a terrorist attack was in progress. Then an explosion was heard and fireworks exploded in the sky over the ruin. The panic subsided and the evening concluded.[48]

More than one published account of the 2,500th anniversary celebrations lists Xenakis as the composer of the music played at the October 15 event. The reasons for this conflation are even more complicated than you might think,[49] but still beg the question of why Xenakis's Polytope de Persépolis was not repeated for the October event, or why he was not commissioned to construct a second *son et lumière*. Perhaps the Shah's advisors feared the appearance of poor diplomacy in inviting the exiled Constantine II of Greece (who did attend) to an event masterminded by the leftist Xenakis. But also, given the rather kitschy nature of the pageantry, Xenakis probably wouldn't have wanted anything to do with it. Whatever the reasons, evidently the Shah and Shahbanu were pleased with everything except the fireworks.[50]

The Shah also knew the event would send a message to his guests that Iran 'could transcend Orientalist traditions and modernize, while at the same time remaining true to Iran's cultural heritage.'[51] And while he may have convinced his guests from abroad that Iran was worth taking seriously, this was among the gestures for which he would soon pay dearly.

8 The Voice of Khomeini

When you take the risk of performing a *gesamtkunstwerk* representing all of Iranian history, its past and future, making use of 130 torch-bearing schoolchildren, gasoline fires and lasers, and a soundtrack of obsessively wrought electroacoustic abstraction, broadcast at high volume to polite, high-heels-wearing society, in the Iranian desert, someone is going to take issue with it. However pure your intentions, the public is going to find—or invent—flaws in them.

The August 28 edition of *Kayhan International* (one of Tehran's English-language newspapers) featured an article entitled 'The Xenakis Attempt to Burn Persepolis.' Its author, the now infamous Amir Taheri (writing pseudonymously as Parisa Parsi), described the music as 'a motley of sounds ranging from thunder to the roar of a jet engine, from caravan bells to the faint echoes of cries of anguish buried under the debris of civilizations to highly abstract noises from the depths of space and time.'[1] Though he meant this to come off as disparaging, it's not entirely inaccurate. Taheri's stronger criticism, however, was the symbology of the polytope. Xenakis's placement of the bonfires at the Naqsh-e Rostam necropolis was at 'exactly the same point Alexander's troops are said to have entered the Apadana, completing their conquest of the Persian empire.'[2] Although Taheri doesn't press the point, the implication is obvious: another Greek come to burn down Persepolis.

Other reviews following the event were more equivocal. The same day, James Underwood, writing in the English-language *Tehran Journal*, comments more on the lack of drinking water at the Persepolis ruin and dry-cleaning services at the Hotel Kurosh.[3] The following day, Taheri (this time writing under his own name) quotes the Shahbanu speaking at a press conference about the event: 'I liked Xenakis's work and I thought the idea was marvellous. All those lights on the hills. This was a unique event that could only happen at Persepolis. But as I said, I am not an authority on the subject. You can dislike it or like it.'[4] In fact, Empress Farah liked the work enough to offer Xenakis the opportunity to design a year-round interdisciplinary center in Shiraz for artists in residence and visitors. (Ultimately, this plan was abandoned.)[5]

A more balanced assessment of the entire affair was published the following week in *Le Nouvel Observateur* by French music journalist Maurice Fleuret, who was present at Persepolis on the night of August 26. In it he praised Xenakis for his having created,

> as usual, an abstract, dense, complex work, the abrupt power of which invests both the senses and the intellect. Despite several technical shortcomings due to disorderly working conditions, this work will serve as a landmark in the evolution of one of the most general and speculative philosophies of our time, with the use of large acoustic spaces and visuals and a human presence within an installation dominated by musical logic. Far from the juvenilia that typically overwhelm historical monuments, Xenakis offers us a model for how to use sound and light.[6]

The real criticism came during a roundtable discussion a few days after the premiere. Amir Taheri was evidently present, as he reported on it in *Kayhan International*.[7] Video and audio recordings capture a tense exchange between Xenakis and Iranian students. In the brief video footage, Xenakis appears exhausted as students level criticisms that *Persepolis* is an insult to Iran, in that the torch-bearing schoolchildren resembled Alexander's Macedonian troops charging down from the hillside and invading the palace. To this, Xenakis and his supporters explained that the fire and lights represented the Zoroastrian values of eternal life and the triumph of good over evil, and the children themselves represented the carriers of these values into tomorrow—a cry of hope for the future—and otherwise, *Persepolis* was absent of narrative.[8] Others lambasted the music itself, saying it could not even be evaluated as good or bad because 'its meaning is the one arbitrarily chosen by its maker'.[9] Someone else decried this lack of symbolic meaning, saying, 'It could have been presented as an homage to a sausage factory.'[10]

Even the students were beginning to turn. For them, *Persepolis* had become a symbol for the unwanted Western influences in Iran, not just in ancient times, but those which the Shah had been perilously importing for decades—those against which they would soon revolt by the millions.

It didn't help that Xenakis, unlike Stockhausen and the others, had a direct connection to the Empress, and thus with the court of the Shah himself. For this reason, Xenakis received some of the most serious criticisms, not from Iranian journalists, who hardly dared to cast aspersion on the Shah's celebrations in the home press, but rather from Iranian expats in Paris who openly characterized the Shah as an oppressive dictator and abuser of human rights. Among these expats were followers of Ayatollah Khomeini, who, in 1971, was still living in exile in Iraq. On November 24, a letter entitled 'L'autre Iran' by Iranian-French author Serge Rezvani (who himself was likely not a supporter of Khomeini) appeared in *Le Monde*, asking how Xenakis (and Peter Brooks) could 'actively be taking part in the happening of Persepolis and endorsing it' when Asadollah Alam, the Iranian minister of the imperial Court, deigns to publicly declare, in whatever context, that 'the peasants must even sell their blankets in order for the festivities to take place.'[11]

Three weeks later, Xenakis responded to Rezvani with an open letter of his own in *Le Monde*. In it he first clarifies that he had no role in the 2,500th anniversary celebrations, per se, only in the Shiraz Arts Festivals, one of which happened to be held a month and a half before the celebrations. He reminds Rezvani that, in fact, he had boldly dedicated *Nuits* (which was performed in Shiraz in 1968) to four unknown political prisoners and thousands of others 'whose names have been erased'— hardly a move made by one who wants to get comfortable with a dictator. He then goes on to explain the meaning of *Persepolis* as a tribute to Iran, her 'Zoroastrian and Manichean revolutionaries' and their gifts to European civilization. What he writes next is very interesting and worth quoting in full:

> 'Democracy' is a lie. What motivated me to go to Iran is this: a deep interest in this magnificent country, so rich with its superposed civilizations and such a hospitable population; the daring adventure of a few friends who founded the Shiraz-Persepolis Festival where all the various tendencies of contemporary, avant-garde art intermingle with the traditional arts of Asia and Africa; plus the warm reception my musical and visual propositions have encountered there by the young members of the general audience. Such a Festival, by the way, partners with our own Festival of Royan, represents a breath of fresh air, don't you think? A good way to spend petrol-dollars, don't you agree?

My philosophy, which I put into practice every day, consists of the freedom of speech, the right to total criticism. I am not an isolationist in a world as tangled and complicated as today's. Therefore, do I preach for an engaged art, meaning a sort of updated 'socialist realism'? Meaning a sort of 'Jdanovian' socialist realism.[12] Obviously not; I am against such an approach. It is imperative to uphold this ultimate right of the individual, especially today when it is impossible to name one single country that is truly free and without multifaceted compromises, without any surrender of principles. 'Democracy' is a fallacy, an artificially sweetened mythology in the mouths of all regimes, be they under the influence of overt dictators or camouflaged ones, throughout the world. Must I couple every country with its own cancer? The United States, with their Vietnam and their treatment of blacks. England, with its treatment of foreigners and the abominable torture of their Irish patriots. Germany and its permanent Nazism. The USSR and its degradation of the freedom to create and think. China and its Maoist religion and its pact with the USA, 'the paper spear-head of worldwide capitalistic imperialism.' … All interchangeable cancers, by the way, between all countries, nations, etc. Where to go in despair, what path may one follow? I am a wandering man, an 'alien citizen' of every country (in art as well) and my hardened conscience—nourished either by the flames of the Greek resistance (which was betrayed from its conception and over the years by the Soviets, the Allies and the Greeks themselves) or by the desperate efforts of my music—alone, may guide me towards light or towards death. For me, the worst and most shameful injustice is the torture and execution (either secretly or overtly) of men and women, even if they are 'terrorists.' This is why I have always been involved, and will continue to be, in protests and actions against dynasties and tyrants, be they military, heads of State, presidents, shahs, or kings. It is in my nature.[13]

Although Mohammad Reza Shah is not called out by name in his letter, the implication is there. It is ironic, then, that *Persepolis* became a symbol for that which Xenakis spent his life fighting against. It must have been painful not just to be generally misunderstood, but to be misperceived as standing for the *opposite* of one's beliefs. This, in addition to Xenakis's growing indignation with the Shah's domestic policies, led him to officially sever his connections to the regime, including the arts center project. In a 1976 letter to Farrokh Ghaffari, the deputy director general of the Shiraz Festival (whom he addresses as 'P. Gaffray'), he wrote:

> You know how attached I am to Iran, her history, her people. You know my joy when I realized projects in your festival, open to everyone. You also know of my friendship and loyalty to those who, like yourself, have made the Shiraz-Persepolis Festival unique in the world. But, faced with inhuman and unnecessary police repression that the Shah and his government are inflicting on Iran's youth, I am incapable of lending any moral guarantee, regardless of how fragile that may be, since it is a matter of artistic creation. Therefore, I refuse to participate in the [1976] festival.[14]

According to Reza Ghotbi, Xenakis also 'had his wife telephone on his behalf to assure the festival directors further that his heart was still with them, despite his inability to continue his work at Shiraz.'[15]

Xenakis was not the only artist to cut ties with the regime. The same year, at a Columbia University event, Iranian novelist and poet Reza Baraheni and British-American playwright

Eric Bentley called for a boycott of the Shiraz Festival based on the Shah's human rights record.[16] Bahareni claims to have spoken with Merce Cunningham, whose dance company was scheduled to take part in the Twelfth Shiraz Arts Festival that year.[17] Pressure on members of the company was coming from other directions as well. Artist Jean Tinguely protested to Gordon Mumma that it was 'immoral to condone a repressive and elitist regime.' To this Mumma counter-argued that 'going to Iran was because of the people and their culture, for which my respect required entering their communities, and learning of their world from their perspective. Their government regime was not their choice.' In the end, Merce Cunningham Dance Company dancer Meg Harper 'spoke eloquently against going, and the decision was made.'[18]

By this time, certain elements in Iran were also taking note of the Festival and its 'avant-garde' material. In 1977, the Squat Theatre, a Hungarian theatre company, performed *Pig, Child, Fire*, an Artaud-inspired play that featured, in its Iranian iteration, a forced sexual encounter, but without nudity.[19] This play was shut down after one performance after a 'respected ayatollah in Shiraz called to complain about the lewd acts reported to him'.[20] But the protest did not stop there.[21] Anthony Parsons, the British ambassador to Iran at the time of the Revolution, recalls

> [t]he effect of this bizarre and disgusting extravaganza on the good citizens of Shiraz, going about their evening shopping, can hardly be imagined. This grotesquerie aroused a storm of protest which reached the press and television. I remember mentioning it to the Shah, adding that, if the same play had been put on, say, in the main street of Winchester (Shiraz is the Iranian equivalent of a cathedral city), the actors and sponsors would have found themselves in trouble. The Shah laughed indulgently.[22]

Ambassador Parsons was bearing witness to the sparks of revolution, which by 1975 would grow as the gap between the rich and poor yawned and widened. Anti-Shah demonstrations were held with increasing regularity by both hardline Islamists and Marxist-leftist elements—strange bedfellows, but effective in concert.[23] For the leftists, the 2,500th celebration epitomized the Shah's 'warped sense of priorities and contempt for common people,' and for the Islamists they were a 'a token of the regime's endemic disdain for Islam and its subservience to the West.' It wasn't just zealots and leftists who questioned the appropriateness of the Festivals for Iran. Some of the Shah's royalist allies 'believe that the festival's avant-garde programmes were partly responsible for many Iranians' alienation from the regime, contributing to its final overthrow.'[24] Even members of Iran's business class, who stood to benefit most from the Shah's Westernization initiatives, stated, 'We were only just beginning to listen to Bach. Stockhausen was impossible.'[25]

It was in this political climate that Jalal Al-e Ahmad, an Iranian novelist and ethnographer, wrote Occidentosis: a Plague from the West (1978), a critique of Western civilization and materialism in general.[26] Drawing on the works of Ernst Jünger, Marx, and Frantz Fanon (whom he met in Paris),[27] Al-e Ahmad defines Gharbzadegi (a Persian neologism perhaps best translated as 'weststruckness') as a contagious disease which requires diagnosis and treatment. Such literature was influential on a class of Iranians disinterested in Khomeini and his sermons, but who nonetheless joined the rallying cries against the court.

Amidst the swelling anti-Shah protests, which spread to Shiraz in 1978, the Twelfth Shiraz Arts Festival program was cancelled, never to be revived.[28] This was a few days before the burning of the Cinema Rex in Abadan, which killed 377 men, women, and children.[29]

English writer William Shawcross summed it up:

> [S]ometimes [the Empress's] enthusiasms seemed to jar. Although she was determined to preserve Iran's past, her contemporary tastes were often too avant-garde, too cosmopolitan, for most of her countrymen.[30]

Among those taking notice of the festival programming was Khomeini. In 1977, while in exile in Najaf, he preached to a crowd of followers,

> You do not know what prostitution has begun in Iran. You are not informed: the prostitution which has begun in Iran, and was implemented in Shiraz—and they say it is to be implemented in Tehran, too—cannot be retold. Is this the ultimate—or can they go even further—to perform sexual acts among a crowd and under the eyes of the people?[31]

Such criticism sounds sincere, and coming from Khomeini it probably was. But as Robert Steele has pointed out, the majority of the Iranian audience, including those present for *Persepolis*, to say nothing of *Pig, Child, Fire*, weren't offended.[32] If the verisimilitude of the festival's theater and the modernism of Xenakis's symbolism got under anyone's skin, it was those who were already convinced that association with the Shah was stigmatic. It was those who were willing to allow the festivals and the 2,500th anniversary celebrations to be used as an excuse for Islamists and leftists to heap aspersion on the Shah.

Perhaps the Shah's greatest single mistake was in referring to Khomeini as a foreigner—the same sort of insult, it turned out, that the students at the roundtable discussion leveled

Figure 11 *A page from* Ettela'at, *January 7, 1978.*

at Xenakis for ostensibly simulating Alexander of Macedon's siege of Persepolis. And for that matter, the language was similar to Khomeini's warnings to his followers about the Shah's internationalism:

> You [the clerics] must be conscripted into compulsory military service, spend your time in jails, under torture and oppression and humiliation, and in exile, so that the way would be open for the agents of the foreigners and of Israel.[33]

The Shah's fatal mistake was publishing an anti-Khomeini article (**left**) in the daily newspaper, *Ettela'at*. Whether it was a direct response to Khomeini's characterization of an Iran run by foreign agents we will never know. 'Iran and Red and Black Colonization,' the article that appeared on January 7, 1978, was aimed at destroying the Khomeini myth, for even in exile his influence had grown too great and his following too devoted for the Shah's comfort. By accusing Khomeini of subservience to colonial powers (without specifying which ones) and pointing out that his grandfather came from India, it could be asked for whose interests this foreigner's grandson, this alien, was working.[34]

When the people of Qom (a city where Khomeini already had a huge popular following) read the article, they grew indignant. They congregated in the streets to discuss the article and those who could read, read it aloud to those who couldn't. The groups increased in size, with new listeners gathering every hour, and eventually the crowd in the main square was massive. No one had given them permission to do this. And then, the most important moment of all: when a policeman approaches the crowd and tells a man to go home, and the man does not go home. As Ryszard Kapuściński wrote, 'The man has stopped being afraid—and this is precisely the beginning of the revolution.' Then policemen later open fire and the dead in the square are wrapped up and buried, and the forty-day mourning period begins, and during that the 'spirit of retaliation and a thirst for revenge seize the people.' And on the fortieth day people gathered in large numbers in Qom and other cities 'to commemorate the victims of the massacre.' Again they were told to disperse and did not, and again they were fired upon, and so the cycle leading to the Revolution with a 'rhythm of explosions succeeding each other at forty-day intervals.' The Shah's response each time was a show of despotic strength because this kind of 'authority attaches great importance to being considered strong, and much less to being admired for its wisdom.'[35]

Meanwhile, storms were gathering in the camps of other opposition groups: the Tudeh Party and other Marxist-Leninist elements, pro-democracy groups such as the Freedom Movement of Iran, and myriad others infuriated by swelling inflation, the squandering of oil profits, and ongoing economic crises.[36]

By this time, 1978, no one was talking about the Shiraz Festivals and the 2,500th anniversary Celebrations anymore. Though they had wetted the ground for the seeds of the Revolution, they were but a pail's worth of the tidal wave that crashed down on the Shah in 1979.

9 Afterlife

The story of *Persepolis* began with Xenakis's electroacoustic work in the studios of Paris and came to an end at the student roundtable discussion in Tehran, and by extension in the pages of *Le Monde*. For the rest of his life, Xenakis composed orchestral and choral works, as well as a few more pieces for tape, but the door he cracked open with *Concret PH* (1958), *Bohor* (1962), *Persepolis* (1971), and *La Légende d'Eer* (1977) was, by 1980, flung wide open by the artists of the Industrial and 'noise' era. With the advent of the portable cassette recorder, artists began recording concrete sounds and voices, looping them, manipulating them, and turning them into music, to reconnoiter the outer bounds of music and express otherwise inarticulable feelings.

Some of these artists (e.g., Merzbow, Rhythm & Noise) have directly cited Philips artists, including Xenakis, as formative. Others, such as Non, Maurizio Bianchi, and Throbbing Gristle, seem to have evolved their tape work without direct influence from Philips artists and their equally important Elektronische Musik contemporaries such as Stockhausen and Gottfried Michael Koenig. Certainly, records by Philips Prospective 21e Siècle artists such as Pierre Henry, Bernard Parmegiani, and Xenakis himself were circulating in Europe, Japan, and the Americas from 1967 on, but to what extent were artists such as Masami Akita, Graeme Revell, and Achim Wollscheid inspired by them? Do I detect, for example, an echo of *Persepolis* in Merzbow's 'Brain Forest' (1990)? Is there something of Xenakis's

Orient-Occident (1960) in Mauizio Bianchi's *Gene-P* (1980)? For Throbbing Gristle and many others, William S. Burroughs was evidently a more important influence than the Philips roster or Stockhausen[1] (but Stockhausen was a guiding light for the Beatles' 'Revolution 9').[2] Xenakis's name even appears on the Nurse with Wound List—does this imply a level of inspiration on the work of Steve Stapleton, et al?[3]

A dissection of Xenakis's influence on contemporary music would be a good topic for a musicology dissertation. James Harley has stated, 'It probably would not be too far wrong to state that most composers of the past 40 years have been influenced in one way or another by [his] music or ideas.'[4] Even if the influence of Xenakis's ideas and work on late-twentieth-century Euro-American classical composition is beyond question, the question of his influence on other forms of music is open. For now, perhaps Alex Reed has summed up as much as we can say:

> There's a vague but deep gut feeling that [20th century classical music and Industrial music] share a fundamental bond—that a hidden truth about industrial music lurks in the oeuvres of Arnold Schoenberg, Iannis Xenakis, and Philip Glass, encoded in the histories of musique concrète and improvisation.[5]

As he implies, drawing genealogical lines around in the arts can be a pointless exercise. Even if we agree with Reed that the influence of Xenakis on popular and unpopular music is palpable, it is also true that cultural diffusion is often indirect, and sometimes innovation is simply 'in the air.'

One artist who attributes direct influence to *Persepolis* is Giancarlo Toniutti. An electronic composer from Udine, Toniutti studied in the early 1980s under Alvise Vidolin at the Venice Conservatory and there heard *Bohor*, which made a great impression on him. A few years later a friend sent him a cassette tape of *Persepolis*. From the experience of listening to *Bohor* and *Persepolis*, he says, a new way of looking at structures emerged:

> I mean in *Persepolis* even more than *Bohor* (which is somehow linearly more homogeneous) the coexistence of various actively dynamic strata constructs a hard matter fully coherent. For me it was this opportunity of having layers which engage in many different modes together (at an angle, at a fold, jumping to a lower layer, sliding into the next structure et cetera) which was one of the most impressive musical realizations of [French mathematician and topologist René] Thom's theoretical work—which I was studying at the time. [Unlike any other work], *Persepolis* has been able to inscribe an 'after' to music composition. With *Persepolis* it is nearly impossible to use any of the previous musicological tools to describe, or analyze, or even think of music. Many of his contemporaries, even though their realizations were important, never reached the point where the sonic matter is so active in itself, beyond any reference to source, to imagination, to literary points of view, et cetera. It is possibly one of the most sonic works ever composed. This coupled with a highly dynamic sound environment, with so many cells, lines, curves, solids, trajectories—highly productive within their inner position in the compositional space. Of course, there also is the interesting performative idea he realized, which adds to the point. [In a more personal way], *Persepolis* and Xenakis in general have taught me to think of density as a fundamental parameter, more so than, say, the gesture/texture of the acousmatic school, or modality in minimalism. Density has become a first step in every

compositional strategy for me. Density is not strictly about thickness, or about the gradient between thickness and thinness, so to say, between heavy compact morphologies and highly sparse forms (between everywhere dense sets and nowhere dense sets). The density parameter strongly affects the behavior of single sounds as well as groups or masses, and in affecting them it opens different views over the generative means through to the sources. As far as I know, only Xenakis has been able to cope with it so significantly well. And I hope to have learnt a bit of that.[6]

Another artist who has found a different kind of inspiration in *Persepolis* is Naut Humon, who co-led Rhythm & Noise, a music and multimedia ensemble that began in 1976 (but had precursors dating back to 1969). R&N presented improvised computer-controlled image and sound collages (or rather, cut-ups). They saw their role not as showmen but as anti-propagandists, finding ways to hack the media control process (another nod to Burroughs).[7] In the bibliography to a c.1983 interview with R&N, conducted by V. Vale and Andrea Juno, Humon lists *Persepolis*, as well as two other Xenakis records.[8] I asked Humon what this record meant to him in his days with R&N as well as more recent work with his CineChamber, a 360° audio and visual experience:

> Xenakis was a central influence on R&N. There is a thread that runs through everything I do. I guess today they call it immersive theater but I call it experiential engineering—the designing of experiences—which comes out of my early days in theater, but the thread I've been following all along, *Persepolis*, was pivotal—pivotal! I felt it on an emotional level, it had a certain surge, a torrential energy that I really liked. The frequencies! As a whole piece, *Persepolis* was a singular

achievement and it continues to inform all that I do today with CineChamber.... The whole idea of space and sound in CineChamber, Xenakis is right there. Also, we did something called Sound Traffic Control in Tokyo with 750 speakers. That was 1991. But the whole idea was to have different musical cargoes and the audience are the passengers from takeoff to touchdown on an imaginary runway in a sonic airport. The whole idea of sound traffic (which later became CineChamber)—the whole idea of panorama in sound comes from Xenakis's work at the World's Fairs and at Persepolis.[9]

On his record label, Asphodel, Humon also released a remix of the original *Persepolis* tapes by Daniel Teruggi. The 2002 CD set included a second disc with shorter interpretations by Otomo Yoshihide, Francisco Lopez, Merzbow, and others, including the late Zbigniew Karkowski, who studied with Xenakis at the Centre Acanthes in France.[10] In fact, it was Karkowski who initiated the reissue.[11] Two years prior, in 2000, Fractal Records released *Persepolis* for the first time on compact disc,[12] which meant for the first time since the premiere the work could be heard as a continuous fifty-five-minute piece. The digital mix for this version was completed by João Rafael at Studio für Elektronische Musik des Instituts für Neue Musik der Staatlichen Hochschule für Musik Freiburg, Breisgau. A version of *Persepolis* was also released as part of a double-CD simply called *Iannis Xenakis* on the Edition RZ label (2003), this time the mixing and remastering was performed by Daniel Teige.[13]

These rereleases all differ slightly from the original Philips LP of *Persepolis*, released in 1972 in France.[14] In theory, the timings of different remixed, remastered versions of a musical work should not differ greatly. And yet, as Reinhold Friedl, composer and proprietor of zeitkratzer Records, noted, the Asphodel version was sixty-one minutes, the Edition RZ edition was just under fifty-one minutes, while the Fractal edition was fifty-five minutes, and the original LP timing was less than forty-seven minutes. How can versions of the same work be timed differently by as much as fourteen minutes? Friedl, who wrote his PhD dissertation on Xenakis's electroacoustic works, deduced first that the Asphodel edition, at over sixty-one minutes, was clearly sampled at an incorrect rate. The Edition RZ version, mixed by Daniel Teige, had a different explanation: in 1971, tape reels had a duration maximum of forty minutes. Because *Persepolis* was longer than forty minutes, for the polytope Xenakis used two machines to overlap the tapes for continuous play. But he never indicated in his notes exactly where the overlapping should begin. Teige opted for a long overlap and shortened the maximum length of the piece by four minutes.[15]

For these reasons, Thomas Herbst's Berlin-based Karlrecords remixed *Persepolis* again for a definitive reissue of all Xenakis's electroacoustic works. I spoke with Herbst about his interest in taking on such a complex work:

> I was impressed how radical and 'modern' it sounded, this was way closer to noise or abstract electronics than most of the Neue Musik of Stockhausen and the likes—that is definitely exciting music too, but always has the feeling of an academic education in it, whereas Xenakis seemed to be from elsewhere, and only later I learned he worked as an architect and was an autodidact. And the electroacoustic music of Xenakis came across very vital and alive, untamed, wild, ferocious … powerful and simply overwhelming.[16]

The idea for the project emerged from a conversation with Friedl. Evidently, *Persepolis* was not the only of Xenakis's works whose recorded versions were sampled at the wrong rate, or even subject to tracks played backward (this was the case particularly with *La Légende D'Eer*). Thus, Friedl wanted to have versions released 'as authentically as possible.'[17] This version of *Persepolis* was included as part of a 2021 quintuple LP boxset featuring Xenakis's complete electroacoustic works.[18]

In May 2019, curator Vali Mahlouji mounted a *Persepolis*-related installation at Berlin's SAVVY Contemporary. *A Utopian Stage* is more than just a nostalgic look back on the Shiraz Arts Festivals. In collecting remnants of the events held in the National Iranian Radio and Television's archives—much of which was destroyed during or after the Revolution—and displaying them alongside publicly available material like artist books and documentaries, the exhibit cut through Western epistemologies about the nature of folk music, classical music, ritual, and theater, just as the Shiraz Festival programming did. Following a nonlinear conceptual map of eastern-western cultural exchange, entitled 'The Shifting Sands of Utopias,' and a film montage of Balinese gamelan performers, a Rwandan drum ensemble, Max Roach, etc., the exhibit traced the trajectory of the Festival, charting its progress as a cultural exchange over the years.[19] Among the video artifacts were excerpts from Pierre Andrégui's documentary film (with English subtitles), which features not only footage of the Polytope de Persépolis, but also interviews with Xenakis at his Corsican summer home and clips of him teaching at Indiana University Bloomington in the early 1970s.[20] For the opening night of *A Utopian Stage*, Mahlouji collaborated with the MaerzMusik festival to broadcast an eight-channel mix of *Persepolis* performed by sound artist and Xenakis researcher Daniel Teige.[21]

Perhaps the most dedicated post-1971 event came in 2010, with the partial reenactment of the Polytope de Persépolis at

Figure 12 *Technicians control the sound experience at the Polytope de Persépolis reenactment, Los Angeles, November 6, 2010.*

State Historic Park in Los Angeles. This event was adapted and re-staged by Daniel Teige. Over a 70,000 square foot region of the park, Teige arranged six listening stations, each with eight speakers, similar to the 1971 event. To capture the visuals, he commissioned a computer-generated light choreography to simulate the lasers, searchlights, fog machines and hazers, bonfires, and torchbearers. The bonfires were staged by a crew from Burning Man and were so hot they could only be sustained for fifteen minutes at a time. On Saturday, November 6, as twilight faded, attendees walked around the park as the light sources shone and the sounds of *Diamorphoses* (the 'geological prelude') and then *Persepolis* filled the darkness, as it had in Iran four decades before.[22] Reviewing this event, one critic referred to Xenakis's music as 'shockingly cold,'[23] but local resident Nancy Cantwell, who attended the event, described it differently: 'I felt *Persepolis* on so many different levels … there was the sense of community, that the music had become subordinate to the experience…. it was mind-bending, historically sweeping, that the antiquities and mysteries of its origins meshed with today's tonalities … an experience that provoked and even moved.'[24]

Notes

Preface

1   The original French lyrics to this song by Resistance leader
    Emmanuel d'Astier de la Vigerie (music by Anna Marley) were
    quite different from the English adaptation by Hy Zaret and
    popularized by Leonard Cohen as 'The Partisan.'

2   Paraphrased from: Sciolino E. 2000. *Persian Mirrors: The Elusive
    Face of Iran*. New York: Free Press, p. 55.

3   Kissinger H. 1979. Kissinger on the Controversy over the
    Shah. *Washington Post,* November 29, p. A-19.

4   Ξενάκη Ι, Θεοδωράκη Μ. 1963. Μία συνομιλία του Ιάννη
    Ξενάκη με τον Μίκη Θεοδωράκη. *Ταχυδρομος* 5/1. https://
    mikisguide.gr/mia-synomilia-tou-ianni-xenaki-me-ton-miki-
    theodoraki/

5   Xenakis I. 1971a. Open letter to *Le Monde*, December 14.
    In: *Music and Architecture: Architectural Projects, Texts, and
    Realizations*. Ed. by Kanach S, 2008 Hillsdale, NY: Pendragon
    Press, p. 224 (translation by Sharon Kanach).

Introduction

1   Payton RJ. 1976. The Music of Futurism: Concerts and
    Polemics. *The Musical Quarterly* 62(1): 33–5.

2   Pratella FB. 1912. *Musica Futurista per Orchestra: Riduzione per
    Pianoforte*. Bologna: Bongiovanni.

3 Moore G. 2019. *The Rite of Spring*. London: Apollo.

4 Boschot A. 1913. Le Sacre du Printemps. Ballet de MM. Roerich, Stravinsky et Nijinsky [*L'Echo de Paris*, 30 mai 1913]. In: *Igor Stravinsky, Le Sacre du Printemps: Dossier de Presse: Press-book*. Ed. by Lesure F, 1980. Gevena: Minkoff (emphasis in original).

5 Lott RA. 1983. 'New Music for New Ears' – The International Composers' Guild. *Journal of the American Musicological Society* 36(2): 266–86.

6 Floros C. 2014. *Alban Berg: Music as Autobiography*. Tr. by Bernhardt-Kabisch E. Frankfurt am Main: Peter Lang GmbH, p. 20; Peterkin N. 1919. Erik Satie's 'Parade.' *The Musical Times* 60(918): 426; Schmidt-Pirro J. 2006. Between the European Avant-garde and American Modernism: George Antheil's 'Ballet Mécanique.' *Soundings: An Interdisciplinary Journal* 89(3/4): 407–8.

7 Boyd H. 2012. Remaking Reality: Echoes, Noise and Modernist Realism in Luigi Nono's 'Intolleranza 1960.' *Cambridge Opera Journal* 24(2): 177–8.

8 Russolo L. 1967 (1913). *The Art of Noise*. New York: Something Else Press, p. 4.

9 ibid., p. 6.

10 Kandinsky V. 1977. *Concerning the Spiritual in Art*. New York: Dover Publications, p. 25.

11 Harrison T. 1996. *1910: The Emancipation of Dissonance*. Berkeley: University of California Press.

12 Potter PM. 2016. *Art of Suppression: Confronting the Nazi Past in Histories of the Visual and Performing Arts*. Oakland: University of California Press.

13 Barron S. 1991. *Degenerate Art. The Fate of the Avant-Garde in Nazi Germany*. Los Angeles: Los Angeles County Museum of Art, p. 17.

14 Attali J. 1985. *Noise: The Political Economy of Music*. Minneapolis: University of Minnesota Press.

15 Matossian N. 1986. *Iannis Xenakis*. New York: Taplinger, p. 125.

16 ibid.

17 ibid., p. 77.

18 Mattis O. 1992. Varèse's Multimedia Conception of 'Déserts.' *The Musical Quarterly* 76(4): 557–83. The insults translate as 'Bastard! Hang him!'

19 Matossian N. 1986, p. 80.

20 ibid.

21 ibid., p. 65.

22 ibid., pp. 55–65.

23 ibid., p. 58.

24 ibid.

Chapter 1

1 Bois M. 1967. *Iannis Xenakis: The Man and His Music*. London: Boosey & Hawkes, p. 10.

2 For recent examples, Organum's *Submission* (1987); Aube's *Spindrift* (1992); or Phill Niblock's *Disseminate* (2004); for examples contemporaneous with Xenakis, works such as *Gesang der Jünglinge* (1955–6) or *Gruppen* (1955–57) by Karlheinz Stockhausen.

3 Matossian N. 1986, pp. 12–14.

4 Varga BA. 1996. *Conversations with Iannis Xenakis*. London: Faber and Faber, p. 7.

5 ibid., pp. 8–10.

6 Matossian N. 1986, pp. 12–14.

7 ibid., pp. 14, 16.

8 Xenakis I. 1980. '[Autobiographical Sketch].' In: *Le fait culturel.* Paris: Fayard, p. 215.

9 Clogg R. 2006. *A Concise History of Greece.* Cambridge: Cambridge University Press, pp. 115–17.

10 Koestler A. 1954. *The Invisible Writing.* New York: Macmillan, p. 376.

11 Clogg R. 2006, pp. 116–18.

12 Matossian N. 1986, pp. 17–18.

13 Xenakis I. 1980, p. 216.

14 Mazower M. 1995. *Inside Hitler's Greece: The Experience of Occupation, 1941–44.* New Haven: Yale University Press, pp. 111–12.

15 Varga BA. 1996, pp. 16–17.

16 Matossian N. 1986, pp. 19–20.

17 Xenakis I. 1980, p. 217.

18 Matossian N. 1986, p. 22.

19 ibid.

20 M.E.P. 1944. Greece and the War. *Bulletin of International News* 21(3): 100.

21 Matossian N. 1986, p. 23.

22 Ioakeim N. 2021. Personal Communication.

23 Iatrides JO. 2015. *Revolt in Athens: The Greek Communist 'Second Round' 1944–1945.* Princeton: Princeton University Press, pp. 158–9.

24 Matossian N. 1986, pp. 23, 25.

25 Iatrides JO. 2015, pp. 171–91.

26 Xenakis I. 1980, pp. 216–17 (translation mine).

27 Later, in conversation with Sharon Kanach, Xenakis referred to Mâkhi as a comrade-in-arms, not a girlfriend.

28 Matossian N. 1986, p. 26.

29 Xenakis I. 1980, p. 217.

30 Matossian N. 1986, p. 25.

31 Clogg R. 2006, pp. 139, 141.

32 Matossian N. 1986, p. 30.

33 Wilson A. 1979. History, Geography and International Law. *The Adelphi Papers* 19(155): 3. See also: Speronis SL. 1955. *The Dodecanese Islands: A Study of European Diplomacy, Italian Imperialism and Greek Nationalism, 1911–1947* [dissertation], p. 221.

34 Varga BA. 1996, pp. 19–20.

35 Matossian N. 1986, p. 30.

Chapter 2

1 Clout H. 2004. Ruins and Revival: Paris in the Aftermath of the Second World War. *Landscape Research* 29(2): 117–39.

2 Laroque G. 1981. La fin des restrictions: 1946–1949. *Economie et Statistique* 129: 5–16.

3 Varga BA. 1996, p. 20. Xenakis says French embassy, but probably means French consul.

4 ibid.

5 Matossian N. 1986, pp. 31–2.

6 Xenakis I. 1980, p. 217.

7 Matossian N. 1986, p. 34.

8   ibid., pp. 35–8.

9   Nouritza Matossian (1986, p. 47) claims this posture was 'as a revenge against his musical mother and brother.'

10 Matossian N. 1986, pp. 47–8.

11 Xenakis I. 1980, p. 218.

12 ibid.

13 Aristotle. 1998. *The Metaphysics*: New York: Penguin. Tr. by Lawson-Tancred H. §1083b. In this translation we read, 'The Pythagoreans, however, say that number is the entities (or at least in applying their theorems they treat bodies as composed of those numbers).'

14 The title of the piece is *Metastaseis* (plural). The original 1966 Le Chant Du Monde release of this album (LDX-A-8368) and all subsequent reissues seem to spell the title *Metastasis* (singular), but this may simply be a French transliteration style. Otherwise, the only exceptions are the Greek versions, which correctly render the title Μεταστάσεις (plural).

15 Xenakis I. 1967. Liner notes to *Metastasis/Pithoprakta/Eonta* (VCS-10030). New York: Vanguard Recording Society.

16 Le Corbusier. 2000. *The Modulor: A Harmonious Measure to the Human Scale, Universally Applicable to Architecture and Mechanics*. Basel: Birkhäuser, pp. 20–1.

17 Harley J. 2004. *Xenakis: His Life in Music*. New York: Routledge, p. 11. See pp. 8–11 of this book for a full technical description of *Metastaseis*.

18 Xenakis I. 1967.

19 Matossian N. 1986, p. 65.

20 Varga BA. 1996, p. 35.

21 ibid.

Chapter 3

1   Judt T. 2006. *Postwar: A History of Europe since 1945*. New York: Penguin Books, p. 226–7

2   Engel FK. 1999. The Introduction of the Magnetophone. In: *Magnetic Recording: The First 100 Years*. Ed. by Daniel ED, et al. New York: Wiley-IEEE Press, p. 48.

3   McMurray P. 2017. Once upon Time: A Superficial History of Early Tape. *Twentieth-Century Music* 14(1): 25–48.

4   Engel FK. 1999, p. 61.

5   Morton DL. 1990. 'John Herbert Orr and the Building of the Magnetic Recording Industry, 1945–1960.' MA thesis, Auburn University, p. 5.

6   Mullin JT. 1972. The Birth of the Recording Industry. *Billboard*, 18 November, p. 56.

7   Morton DL. 1990. John Herbert Orr and the Building of the Magnetic Recording Industry, 1945–1960. http://aes-media.org/historical/pdf/morton_john-herbert-orr.pdf.

8   McMurray P. 2017, p. 42.

9   Leslie J, Snyder R. 2010. History of the Early Days of Ampex Corporation. https://www.aes.org/aeshc/docs/company.histories/ampex/leslie_snyder_early-days-of-ampex.pdf.

10 Hodgkinson T. 1987. An Interview with Pierre Schaeffer, Pioneer of Musique Concrète. *ReR Quarterly* 2(1): 3. It is interesting to hear Schaeffer say he had formal musical training since, years before, when Xenakis's score for *Anastenaria* (1952–4) arrived at his studio, he claimed he could not read music and had to have Pierre Henry study it.

11 Schaeffer P. 2010. *Essai sur la radio et le cinéma. Esthétique et technique des arts-relais, 1941–1942*. Paris: Éditions Allia, pp. 47–54.

12 Palombini C. 1993. Machine Songs V: Pierre Schaeffer: From Research into Noises to Experimental Music. *Computer Music Journal* 17(3): 14.

13 Schaeffer P. 1952. *A la Recherche d'une Musique Concrete*. Paris: Editions du Seuil, pp. 18–19. (Published in English as: Schaeffer P. 2012. *In Search of a Concrete Music*. Berkeley: University of California Press).

14 Dixon J. 2000. *Electro-acoustic Music Pre-1960: Historicity and Ideology* [dissertation], Durham University, pp. 74–5.

15 Collins N. 2013. The Post-war Sonic Boom. In: *Electronic music*. Ed. by Collins N, Schedel M, Wilson S. Cambridge: Cambridge University Press, p. 46. Also see Palombini 1993, p. 15.

16 Dixon J. 2000, p. 77.

17 ibid.

18 The notable exception is Egyptian composer Halim El-Dabh, who in 1944 recorded a *zar* (exorcism) ceremony with a magnetic wire recorder borrowed from Middle East Radio in Cairo. He also later experimentally manipulated the recording at the radio studio before transferring it to magnetic tape. See Holmes T. 2008. *Electronic and Experimental Music: Technology, Music, and Culture*. 3rd edition. New York: Routledge, p. 156. Also, in 1939 John Cage produced *Imaginary Landscape No. 1*, a piece for two variable-speed turntables, frequency recordings, piano, and Chinese cymbal. See Lange A. Liner notes to *Imaginary Landscapes* [hat ART CD 6179].

19 Dixon J. 2000, p. 75.

20 Collins N. 2013, pp. 46–7.

21 ibid., pp. 49–50. See also Holmes T. 2008. *Electronic and Experimental Music: Technology, Music, and Culture.* 3rd edition. New York: Routledge, pp. 56–61.

22 Hodgkinson T. 1987, pp. 8–9.

23 ibid., pp. 4. 8–9.

24 Dixon J. 2000, p. 81. More generally, see Kurtz M. 1992. *Stockhausen: A Biography.* London and Boston: Faber and Faber; and Morawska-Büngeler M. 1988. *Schwingende Elektronen. Eine Dokumentation über das Studio für Elektronische Musik des Westdeutschen Rundfunks in Köln 1951–1986.* Cologne-Rodenkirchen: P.J. Tonger.

25 Palombini C. 1999. Musique Concrète Revisited. *Electronic Musicological Review* 4: 4–5. See also Dixon J. 2000, p. 77.

26 Hodgkinson T. 1987, p. 9.

27 Matossian N. 1986, p. 76.

28 ibid., pp. 76–7.

29 Harley J. 2004, p. 17.

30 Varga BA. 1996, p. 111.

31 ibid.

32 Matossian N. 1986, p. 110.

33 ibid.

34 Kalia R. 1987. *Chandigarh: The Making of an Indian City.* New Delhi: Oxford University Press, pp. 70–120.

35 Matossian N. 1986, pp. 111–21.

36 Nobody knows for sure what the 'PH' in *Concret PH* stands for. It may simply be short for 'Philips'; another suggestion is 'paraboloid hyperboloid.'

37 Delalande F. 1998. '*Il faut être constamment un immigré':
    entretiens avec Xenakis*. Paris: Buchet Chastel, p. 36. See also
    Matossian N. 1986, pp. 121–2.

38 Zouhar V, et al. 2005. Proposals have been made for a
    virtual reconstruction of the Poème Électronique, if not the
    Philips Pavilion itself. See Lombardo V, et al. 2009. A Virtual-
    Reality Reconstruction of Poème Électronique Based on
    Philological Research. *Computer Music Journal* 33(2): 24–47.
    See also: Hearing Varèse's Poème Électronique Inside a
    Virtual Philips Pavilion. *International Conference on Auditory
    Display, 2005 [Proceedings of ICAD 05 - Eleventh Meeting of the
    International Conference on Auditory Display, Limerick, Ireland,
    July 6–9, 2005]*. Atlanta, GA: Georgia Institute of Technology
    International Community for Auditory Display, pp. 247–8.

39 Treib M. 1996. *Space Calculated in Seconds: The Philips Pavilion,
    Le Corbusier, Edgard Varèse*. Princeton: Princeton University
    Press, pp. 34–7.

40 Clarke J. 2012. Iannis Xenakis and the Philips Pavilion. *The
    Journal of Architecture* 17(2): 217.

41 Kıyak A. 2003. *Describing the Ineffable: Le Corbusier, Le Poème
    Electronique and Montage* [dissertation]. Wissenschaftliche
    Zeitschrift der Bauhaus-Universität Weimar, pp. 161–3.
    See also Clarke J. 2012, pp. 216–17 and Matossian N. 1986,
    p. 122.

42 Treib M. 1996, pp. 188–91. See also the liner notes for *Poème
    Electronique and Other Selections* [EAV Lexington MAS 4237].

43 Matossian N. 1986, p. 211.

44 Xenakis I. 1976. *Musique - Architecture*. 2nd edition. Paris:
    Casterman, p. 143 (translation mine).

45 Ibid., pp. 143–4.

Chapter 4

1 Kuhrt A. 1983. The Cyrus Cylinder and Achaemenid Imperial Policy. *Journal for the Study of the Old Testament* 25: 84–7.

2 Steele R. 2021. *The Shah's Imperial Celebrations of 1971: Nationalism, Culture and Politics in Late Pahlavi Iran*. London: I.B. Taurus, p. 44.

3 *United Nations Press Release 14 October 1971* (SG-SM-1553-HQ263).

4 Steele R. 2021, p. 27.

5 Leroy M. 1974. Éternel Iran. In: *Commémoration Cyrus. Actes du Congrès de Shiraz 1971 et Autres Études Rédigées à L'occasion du 2500ᵉ Anniversaire de la Fondation de L'empire Perse. Volume I: Hommage Universel*. Leiden: Brill, p. 24. (Partial English translation found in: Kuhrt A. 1983, p. 84. Remaining translation mine).

Even if these statements were made with some amount of flattery for the Shah in mind, and even if referring to the Cyrus Cylinder as a human rights declaration involves some creativity, it has more plausibly been suggested that the Cylinder influenced even the American Founding Fathers, since, as historian Richard Frye points out, Jefferson owned a copy (two copies, in fact) of Xenophon's *Cyropaedia*, a biography of Cyrus the Great. See Frye R, Zand A. 2013. *Jefferson and Cyrus: How the Founding Fathers of America, in Their Own Words, Were Inspired by Cyrus the Great* (Synopsis of Upcoming Book). www.richardfrye.org.

6 Busnel J. 1971. The 2,500th Anniversary of the Foundation of the Persian Empire Will Be Celebrated This Coming October 15th. Unpublished document. Iannis Xenakis Archives OM

27-4-2. Xenakis did not attend the October events, despite having received this literature, presumably along with an invitation.

7 Connections between the August Shiraz Festival and the main celebrations in October were perhaps less ideological and more logistical (the same Philips sound equipment and other infrastructure were used for both); it was the Year of Cyrus and Xenakis's piece was about Persian history.

8 Meyers EM, Burt S. 2010. Exile and Return: From the Babylonian Destruction to the Beginnings of Hellenism. In: *Ancient Israel: from Abraham to the Roman Destruction of the Temple*. Ed. by Shanks H. 3rd edition. Washington DC: Biblical Archaeology Society, pp. 217–24.

It is worth pointing out, however, that the Cyrus Cylinder mentions neither Judah nor Jerusalem. So, while it may be evidence of a general policy of allowing deportees to return and to re-establish cult sites, it doesn't actually say anything about freeing the Israelites; only the Old Testament says this.

9 Steele R. 2021, p. 14.

10 ibid., p. 16.

11 ibid., p. 17.

12 Fallaci O. 1976. *Interview with History*. Boston: Houghton Mifflin, p. 286.

13 Shah Pahlavi MR. 1961. *Mission for My Country*. London: Hutchinson & Co., p. 18.

14 Marashi A. 2008. *Nationalizing Iran*. Seattle: University of Washington Press, p. 89.

15 Wilber DN. 1975. *Reza Shah Pahlavi: The Resurrection and Reconstruction of Iran*. Hicksville: Exposition Press, p. 98.

16 Mousavi A. 2012. *Persepolis: Discovery and Afterlife of a World Wonder*. Boston: Walter de Gruyter, p. 144.

17 Steele R. 2021, p. 22.

18 Shakibi Zh. 2020. *Pahlavi Iran and the Politics of Occidentalism: The Shah and the Rastakhiz Party*. London: I.B. Tauris.

19 Hambly GRG. 1991. The Pahlavī Autocracy: Riżā Shāh, 1921–1941. In: *The Cambridge History of Iran. Volume 7: From Nadir Shah to the Islamic Republic*. Ed. by Avery P, Hambly G, Melville C. Cambridge: Cambridge University Press, pp. 232–3. See also Sanasarian E. 2000. *Religious Minorities in Iran*. Cambridge: Cambridge University Press, pp. 46–8.

20 Marashi A. 2008, pp. 79–85.

21 Hambly GRG. 1991, p. 283.

22 Shah Pahlavi MR. 1961, p. 13.

23 ibid., p. 28.

24 Pahlavi F. 2004. *An Enduring Love: My Life with the Shah*. New York: Miramax, p. 72.

25 Siamdoust N. 2017. *Soundtrack of the Revolution: The Politics of Music in Iran*. Stanford: Stanford University Press, p. 46.

26 Minu-Sepehr A. 2012. *We Heard the Heavens then: A Memoir of Iran*. New York: Free Press, p. 73.

27 Kapuściński R. 1992. *Shah of Shahs*. New York: Vintage International, pp. 52–60.

28 Shah Pahlavi MR. 1961, p. 132.

29 Bassett SR. 1999. The Death of Cyrus the Younger. *The Classical Quarterly* 49(2): 477–8. See also Avery HC. 1972. Herodotus' Picture of Cyrus. *American Journal of Philology* 93(4): 529–46.

30 Plato. 1961. *Laws*. Book III. Loeb Classical Library. Tr. by Bury JG. Cambridge: Harvard University Press, pp. 225, 227, 231.

31 Steele R. 2021, p. 24.

Chapter 5

1   Shah Pahlavi MR. 1961, p. 190.

2   ibid., p. 320.

3   The Arabic root word 'nesf' (نصف) implies bisection into equal divisions. A less faithful but more wholesome translation might be 'Isfahan is the center of the world.'

4   Sreberny-Mohammadi A, Mohammadi A. 1994. *Small Media Big Revolution: Communication, Culture and the Iranian Revolution*. Minneapolis: University of Minnesota Press, p. 72.

5   Pahlavi F. 2004, pp. 227–8.

6   Gluck R. 2007. The Shiraz Arts Festival: Western Avant-Garde Arts in 1970s Iran. *Leonardo* 40(1): 21.

7   Chehabi HE. 2018. The Shiraz Festival and Its Place in Iran's Revolutionary Mythology. In: *The Age of Aryamer: late Pahlavi Iran and Its Global Entanglements*. Ed. by Alvandi R. London: Gingko Library, p. 168.

8   ibid., p. 170.

9   Pahlavi F. 2004, p. 228.

10 Gluck R. 2007, p. 22.

11 Wilson R. 2013. Ka Mountain and GUARDenia Terrace: A Story about a Family and Some People Changing, a 168 Hour Play for the 1972 Festival of Shiraz. In: *Iran Modern*. Ed. By Daftari F, Diba LS. New Haven: Yale University Press, pp. 93–5. See also: Shyer L. 1989. *Robert Wilson and His Collaborators*. New York: Theatre Communications Group, pp. 34–63.

12 Pahlavi F. 2004, p. 233.

13 ibid., p. 228. For general information on the genres and styles of Persian classical music concerned here,

consult: Chelkowski P. 1991. Popular Entertainment, Media and Social Changes in 20th Century Iran. In: *The Cambridge History of Iran, Vol. 7: From Nadir Shah to the Islamic Republic.* Cambridge: Cambridge University Press, pp. 765–814; Nettl B. 1970. Attitudes towards Persian Music in Tehran, 1969. *The Musical Quarterly* 56(2): 183–97; Zonis E. 1973. *Classical Persian Music: An Introduction.* Cambridge: Harvard University Press.

14 Gluck R. 2007, p. 22.

15 Pahlavi F. 2004, p. 232.

16 ibid., p. 233.

17 Besançon H. 2007. *Festival international d'art contemporain de Royan 1964–1977.* Vaux-sur-Mer: Éditions Bonne Anse, p. 23.

18 Underwood J. 1969. 'Noise' Musicians Must Also be Gifted! *Kayhan International*, September 11, p. 8.

19 Interestingly, this was the production company that helped finance Orson Welles's *F Is for Fake* and *The Other Side of the Wind*. As those who followed Welles's career will know, these deals did not end well. See: McBride J. 2006. *What Ever Happened to Orson Welles? A Portrait of an Independent Career.* Lexington: University Press of Kentucky, pp. 202–7. Connected to this, Xenakis's percussion piece *Psappha* was blended into the soundtrack of *The Other Side of the Wind*. See: Kanach S. 2014. Xenakis et le Film: La Face Cachée du Compositeur. In: *Xenakis et les Arts: Miscellanées.* Ed. By Kanach S. Rouen: Éditions Point de Vues, p. 139.

20 Restagno E. 1988. *Xenakis.* Torino: EDT/Musica, p. 40 (translation mine). In September 1970, Boushehri was promoted to head of the Central Council for the

Celebrations, replacing his uncle Javad Boushehri, who was undergoing treatment for cancer. Furthermore, he was living in Paris at the time and could not be directly involved with planning at the site. See: Ansari A. 2017. *The Shah's Iran: Rise and Fall: Conversations with an Insider*. London: I.B. Tauris, p. 249. According to Abdolreza Ansari, the idea for the celebrations was originally proposed by an Iranian scholar named Shojaeddin Shafa. See Kadivar C. 2002. We Are Awake: 2,500-year Celebrations Revisited. *The Iranian*, January 25. Farah Pahlavi, in her memoirs, also cites Shafa as one who conceived of the idea. See Pahlavi F. 2004, p. 213.

21 Various sources claim the source languages were Sumerian, Assyrian, Achaean, ancient Persian, and so on. About this, Xenakis wrote, 'My intention was, on the contrary, to develop a work based on these very elements of language. What fascinated me in Doblhofer's book, is that it shows that all syllabic alphabets were based on consonants and not on vowels. On page 271, I discovered the Mycenæan syllabary [Linear-B], and the Sumerian and Persian scripts.' See Julien J-R. 1986. *Nuits* d'Iannis Xenakis: Éléments d'une analyse. *L'Éducation Musicale 325*, p. 6 (translation by Sharon Kanach). By 'Doblhofer's book' he means Austrian philologist Ernst Doblhofer's *Zeichen und Wunder. Die Entzifferung alter Schriften und Sprachen* (1957), translated and published in English in as *Voices in Stone: The Decipherment of Ancient Scripts and Writings* (1961). See also: Ioakeim N. 2022. *From Alpha to Omega: The Titles of Iannis Xenakis*. Hillsdale: Pendragon Press (forthcoming).

22 Xenakis I. 1973. *Nuits: musique pour 12 voix mixtes*. Paris: Éditions Salabert. This dedication appears in the Forward.

23 Xenakis I. 1971a, p. 223 (translation by Sharon Kanach).

24 Persephassa is an alternate name for the Greek goddess Persephone, daughter of Demeter and Zeus. While picking flowers in a meadow she was abducted by Hades, god of the underworld, with the consequence that she must divide her year between the upper world and the underworld realm. Thus, her return in spring is associated with telluric forces and fertility, and her return to the underworld with the coming of winter. For a description of the myth, see Hornblower S, et al, eds. 2012. *The Oxford Classical Dictionary*, 4th edition, pp. 1109–10. Although 'Persephone' (Περσεφόνη) and 'Persepolis' (Περσέπολις) sound like they would have a common root word, there is no apparent etymological connection, the former seemingly arising from an Indo-European word for grain (Beekes R. 2010. *Etymological Dictionary of Greek*. Leiden: Brill, pp. 1179–80) and the latter related to the ethnonym Pars for Persian, itself of uncertain origin, though likely from Sanskrit (Hoffmann K. 1940. Vedische Namen. *Wörter und Sachen* 21, p. 142).

25 Harley J. 2004, p. 60.

26 The word *polytope* combines the Greek words *polys* (πολύς), meaning 'many,' and *topos* (τόπος), meaning 'places.'

27 Xenakis I. 1976, p. 159 (translation mine).

28 ibid., p. 160.

29 d'Allonnes OR. 1975. *Xenakis: les Polytopes*. Paris: Balland, p. 19 (translation mine).

30 Varga BA. 1996, p. 112.

31 ibid., pp. 112–13.

32 ibid., p. 114.

33 Harley MA. 1998. Music of Sound and Light: Xenakis's Polytopes. *Leonardo* 31(1): 56–7.

34 Pahlavi F. 2004, p. 233.

Chapter 6

1 No author. [1971]. *A Glance at Persepolis, Pasargadae, Naqsh-e Rostam, Naqsh-e Rajab.* Tehran: Sekeh Press, pp. 31–2.

2 Harley J. 2002. The Electro-acoustic Music of Iannis Xenakis. *Computer Music Journal* 26(1): 46–7. Xenakis may have recorded some of these sounds himself in the studio (or perhaps even borrowed from the studio sound library), but he doesn't tell us which ones.

3 Teige D. 2012. Dead or Alive. Aspects Concerning the Performance and Interpretation of Xenakis's Polytopes Today. In: *Xenakis Matters: Contexts, Processes, Applications.* Ed. by Kanach S. Hillsdale, NY: Pendragon Press, p. 249.

4 ibid., pp. 250–1.

5 Xenakis I. 1971b. *«Persepolis» Spectacle and Music* [program notes]. Tehran: s.n. Reproduced in: Kanach S, ed. 2008. *Music and Architecture: Architectural Projects, Texts, and Realizations.* Hillsdale, NY: Pendragon Press, pp. 221–2.

6 ibid., p. 248. These master tapes, and Xenakis's scores, are today held by the Archives de Iannis Xenakis in Paris. The first reel contains lambda elements 1, 2, 3, 5, and 6. The second reel contains 7, 8, 9, 10, and 11. (Xenakis does not offer an explanation as to why he bypassed numeral 4).

7 ibid., pp. 248–9.

8   No author. 1971. Studio Acousti Enregistrements Sonore Tarifs 1971. Unpublished document. Archives de Iannis Xenakis OM 27-4-2.

9   Teige D. 2012, pp. 246–7.

10 ibid., p. 247.

11 ibid., pp. 247–8.

12 Hollande E. 2014. *Louis Dufay, la Couleur et l'Héliophore*. https://vimeo.com/133017858. Accessed November 19, 2021.

13 Kharamzi M. 1971. World premiere of 'Persepolis' by Xenakis. *Kayhan International*, August 17: 6.

14 Xenakis I. 1971a, p. 223.

15 The prophet's name, which has come down to us from Avestan as Zarathustra, has been interpreted numerous ways, most of which involve management of camels. For a discussion, see: https://iranicaonline.org/articles/zoroaster-i-the-name. As far as the 'living star' interpretation of the Greek version 'Zoroaster,' this comes from Gregory of Tours, apparently in turn drawing on an interpretation associated with Pope Clement I. See Jackson AVW. 1899. *Zoroaster, the Prophet of Ancient Iran*. New York: Macmillan, pp. 125–6, 238–9, 250. Alternately, De Jong, drawing on Aristotle, suggests the meaning is in fact 'star worshipper,' i.e., astrologer. See De Jong A. 1997. *Traditions of the Magi: Zoroastrianism in Greek and Latin Literature*. Leiden: Brill, p. 212.

16 Boyce M. 2001. *Zoroastrians: Their Religious Beliefs and Practices*. London: Routledge, pp. 26, 42.

17 Jackson AVW. 1899. *Zoroaster, the Prophet of Ancient Iran*. London: Macmillan & Co., Ltd., pp. 62–4.

18 Xenakis I. 1971a, p. 224.

19 Boyce M. 2001, p. 26.

20 Skjærvø PO. 2005. *An Introduction to Zoroastrianism*. PDF booklet for use in Early Iranian Civilizations 102 (Harvard Divinity School no. 3663a), p. 18.

21 *Yasna* 51:9. See: Mills LH. 1887. *The Zend-Avesta. Part III: The Yasna, Visparad, Afrînagân, Gâhs, and Miscellaneous Fragments*. Oxford: Clarendon Press, pp. 181–2. For a rather different interpretation of this passage (albeit translated into German), see: Lommel H. 1930. *Die Religion Zarathustras nach dem Awesta dargestellt*. Tübingen: Mohr, p. 291.

22 Baker-Brian NJ. 2011. *Manichaeism: An Ancient Faith Rediscovered*. London: T&T Clark International, pp. 110–13. Another version is found in Widengren G. 1961. *Mani and Manichaeism*. Tr. by Kessler C. London: Weidenfeld and Nicolson, pp. 49–52.

23 Hesiod. 2006. *Theogony* §507–613 & *Works and Days* §42–105. Tr. by Most GW. Loeb Classical Library. Cambridge: Harvard University Press.

24 Kharazmi M, World Premiere of 'Persepolis' by Xenakis. *Kayhan International*, August 17, 1971, p. 6.

25 Kia M. 1998. Persian Nationalism and the Campaign for Language Purification. *Middle Eastern Studies* 34(2): 18.

26 Xenakis I. 1971, p. 224.

Chapter 7

1 Kanach S. 2008. The Polytope de Persépolis 1971. In: *Music and Architecture: Architectural Projects, Texts, and Realizations*. Ed. by Kanach S. Hillsdale, NY: Pendragon Press, p. 219.

2 An August 17 newspaper article states Xenakis was already in Iran on this date. See Kharamzi M. 1971, p. 6.

3 What looks like a stanchioned speaker is visible briefly in Pierre Andrégui's 1971 film, *Xenakis: Persepolis*. Paris: Sodaperaga.

4 Kanach S, ed. 2008, p. 222. Nothing more is known about the identity of these crewmembers, except that it is possible we catch a glimpse of them in Andrégui's film.

5 An additional three minutes can be glimpsed in Naser Taghvai's [spelled Nasser Taqvai in the credits] documentary short, seemingly titled *Persepolis/Iannis Xenakis*. Since a cameraman (M. Zarfam) is credited, it is presumed he and Andrégui were working separately at the event.

6 No author. 1971. *Fifth Festival of Arts Shiraz-Persepolis Programme*. s.l.: s.n.

7 ibid.

8 Kanach S. 2008, p. 219.

9 Fleuret M. 1971. L'anti-son et lumière. *Nouvel Observateur* 356: 43. (It is possible that only excerpts of *Diamorphoses* were played that night.)

10 Kanach S. 2008, pp. 219–20.

11 ibid., p. 221.

12 Fleuret M. 1971, p. 43.

13 Kanach S. 2008, p. 219.

14 ibid., pp. 219–20.

15 ibid., p. 219.

16 Gorguin I, ed. 1971. *5th Festival of Arts Shiraz-Persepolis*. Shiraz: Public Relations Bureau of the Festival of the Arts, p. 100.

17 ibid.

18 Steele R. 2021, pp. 26–7.

19 Afkhami GR. 2009. *The Life and Times of the Shah*. Berkeley: University of California Press, p. 421.

20 Gluck R. 2013. A New East-West Synthesis: Conversations with Iranian Composer Alireza Mashayekhi. *eContact!* 14(4). https://econtact.ca/14_4/gluck_mashayekhi.html

21 No author. c. 2002. *Jashn-i Hunar-i Shīrāz bih rivāyat-i asnād-i Sāvāk* [The Shiraz Art Festival according to SAVAK documents]. Tehran: Markaz-i Bar'rasī-i Asnād-i Tārīkhī-i Vizārat-i Ittilā'āt [Center of Historical Documents Survey, Ministry of Intelligence]. Thanks to Houchang Chehabi for his interpretation and commentary on these texts.

22 Steele R. 2021, pp. 43–4.

23 Milani A. 2011. *The Shah*. New York: Palgrave Macmillan, p. 323.

24 Pahlavi F. 2004, pp. 221–2.

25 No Author. 1971. Banquet of the Century. *Kayhan International*, October 23, p. 3. See also: Pahlavi F. 2004, pp. 218–19.

26 Steele R. 2021, pp. 43–6.

27 ibid., p. 40.

28 Curtis C. 1971. Tent City Awaits Celebration: Shah's 'Greatest Show.' *New York Times*, October 12, p. 39.

29 ibid., pp. 39–40.

30 ibid., p. 40.

31 No author. 1978. Maxim's Is Dropped from the 1978 Michelin Guide. *New York Times*, March 7, p. 41.

32 Milani A. 2011, p. 325.

33 ibid., p. 326.

34 Ansari A. 2017. *The Shah's Iran: Rise and Fall: Conversations with an Insider.* London: I.B.Tauris & Co., p. 267.

35 Curtis C. 1971. p. 39.

36 Mulchrone V. 1971. The Biggest Beano since Babylon … *Daily Mail*, October 11, p. 6. 'Kipper' is British slang for herring. No herring was served at the banquet.

37 Milani A. 2011, p. 325.

38 ibid., p. 323.

39 Milani A. 2011, p. 325.

40 Steele R. 2021, p. 47. The Shah was famously allergic to caviar and so was served something else. See: Cooper A. 2016. *The Fall of Heaven: The Pahlavis and the Final Days of Imperial Iran.* New York: Henry Holt and Company, pp. 19, 558.

41 Milani A. 2011, p. 325.

42 Ansari A. 2017, p. 258.

43 Elwell-Sutton LP. 1971. [On the 2500th Anniversary Celebrations.] *Bulletin of the British Association of Orientalists* 6: 20–5.

44 Tjeknavorian L. 2021. Personal communication. The soundtrack to the evening is available on the records listed here: https://www.discogs.com/release/3335808-Loris-Z-Tjeknavorian-Persepolis and here: https://www.discogs.com/release/6960883-Loris-Z-Tjeknavorian-Son-Et-Lumiere-Persepolis.

45 Taheri M. Persepolis Son et Lumiere: Spectacles in Diplomacy [unpublished dissertation manuscript].

46 Steele R. 2021, p. 48.

47 Taheri M. [unpublished dissertation manuscript].

48 Kadivar C. 2002. (Kadivar is, for these details, recounting a conversation he had with Abdolreza Ansari).

49 Those interested in the political machinations behind the conflation are encouraged to consult Mehdi Taheri's dissertation (which he graciously permitted me to review prior to its defense), as well as his Persian-language article, Tjeknavorian's Son et Lumiere vs Xenakis's Polytope: Racism and the Historiography of Music in Modern Iran. *Mahoor Quarterly* (Under Review).

50 Reported by Abdolreza Ansari in an interview with Manoto TV. Ansari, a member of the 2,500th anniversary celebrations council, recounts a conversation between the Shahbanu and someone (it is unclear who), wherein the Shahbanu asks whose silly idea the fireworks were, to which her interlocutor replies, 'It was mine and I am sure everyone enjoyed it.' Thanks to Mehdi Taheri for help with translation.

51 Grigor T. 2005. Preserving the Antique Modern: Persepolis '71. *Future Anterior* 2(1): 26.

Chapter 8

1 Parsi P. 1971. The Xenakis Attempt to Burn Persepolis. *Kayhan International,* August 28, p. 6.

2 ibid.

3 Underwood J. 1971. Xenakis Reverberates through Shiraz Hills. *Tehran Journal,* August 28, pp. 1, 8.

4 Taheri A. 1971. Empress Defends Celebration as National Target. *Kayhan International,* August 29, p. 4.

5 Gluck R. 2007, pp. 25–6.

6 Fleuret M. 1971, p. 43 (translation mine).

7 Khavari M. 1971. Persepolis' Controversy a Greek Fury. *Kayhan International,* August 30, p. 6.

8 ibid. See also: Kanach S. 2008, p. 218.

9 ibid.

10 ibid.

11 Rezvani S. 1971. L'autre Iran. *Le Monde*, November 24, p. 6 (translation mine).

12 Xenakis is here referring to a post-War Soviet cultural policy that allowed strict government control to be exerted over art and intellectual activity. He spells it 'Jdanovian' but it is usually transliterated as Zhdanovism (for Andrey Aleksandrovich Zhdanov). See: Swayze H. 2013. *Political Control of Literature in the USSR, 1946–1959*. Cambridge: Harvard University Press, pp. 26–82.

13 Xenakis I. 1971a, pp. 223–4 (translation by Sharon Kanach).

14 Xenakis I. 1976. [*Letter to P. Gaffray*]. Reproduced in Kanach S. 2008, p. 161 (translation by Sharon Kanach).

15 Afkhami GR. 2009.

16 No author. 1976. Iran Accused at Meeting Here of Torture and Repression. *New York Times*, February 29, p. 5. See also: Navasky VS. 1976. The Moral Question Boycott—the Political Question, the Practical Question. *New York Times*, August 15, pp. 11, 15, 17, 20.

17 Baraheni R. 1976. Iran Boycott: An Exchange. *New York Review of Books*, November 25, p. 46.

18 Gluck R. 2007, p. 26.

19 Afkhami GR. 2009, pp. 418–19. Curiously, this description by Farrokh Ghaffari does not match another description of the play found in: Shank T. 1977. Squat's 'Pig, Child, Fire!' *The Drama Review* 21(3): 95–100.

20 Afkhami GR. 2009, p. 419.

21 Houshang Chebahi cites several other examples of avant-garde theater featured at previous Festivals (e.g., Victor García's production of Jean Genet's *Les Bonnes*, Grotowski's staging of Calderón de la Barca's *The Constant Prince*) that likely contributed to an 'association with immorality in the minds of traditionalist Iranians.' See: Chehabi HE. 2018. The Shiraz Festival and Its Place in Iran's Revolutionary Mythology. In: *The Age of Aryamer: Late Pahlavi Iran and Its Global Entanglements*. Ed. by Alvandi R. London: Gingko Library, p. 176.

22 Parsons A. 1984. *The Pride and the Fall: Iran, 1974–1979*. London: Jonathan Cape, pp. 54–5.

23 Ghazvinian J. 2021. *America and Iran: A History, 1720 to the Present*. New York: Alfred A. Knopf, pp. 313–14.

24 Chehabi HE. 2018, p. 168.

25 Shawcross W. 1988. *The Shah's Last Ride: Fate of an Ally*. New York: Simon and Schuster, pp. 97–8.

26 Al-e Ahmad J. 1984. *Occidentosis: A Plague from the West*. Tr. by Cambell R. Berkeley: Mizan Press. This polemical book was originally self-published in Tehran in 1978. Part of it were presented to the Congress on the Aim of Iranian Education as early as 1961, at which time draft typescripts were circulated privately.

27 Algar H. 1982. Introduction. In: Al-e Ahmad J. 1984. *Occidentosis: A Plague from the West*. Tr. by Cambell R. Berkeley: Mizan Press, pp. 15, 17.

28 Shakibi Zh. 2020, p. 294. Aside from the political pressures to cancel the 1978 festival, the Shah's cancer was by this point advancing rapidly (Keddie 2006: 215), and this may also have influenced the decision.

29 Amanat A. 2017. *Iran: A Modern History*. New Haven: Yale University Press, p. 716. The number of dead in the Cinema Rex fire ranges from 377 to 470 in various sources.

30 Shawcross W. 1988, p. 97.

31 Arjomand SA. 1984. Traditionalism in Twentieth-century Iran. In: *From Nationalism to Revolutionary Islam*. Ed. by Arjomand SA. London: Macmillan, pp. 224–5. This speech made by Khomeini is attributed to 14 Shawwal 1397 A.H., which would be September 28, 1977. Another version of this same speech adds the phrasing 'The gentlemen [clerics] in Iran don't say anything. I cannot understand why they don't speak out!' See: Gluck R. 2007, p. 27.

32 Steele R. 2021. Personal communication.

33 Arjomand SA. 1984, p. 225.

34 Shahidi H. 2007. *Journalism in Iran: From Mission to Profession*. New York: Routledge, pp. 9–10.

35 Kapuściński R. 1985, pp. 106–15.

36 Milani A. 2011, pp. 296, 300–1, 384; Keddie N. 2006. *Modern Iran: Roots and Results of Revolution*. New Haven: Yale University Press, p. 216.

Chapter 9

1 Vale V, Juno A. 1983. *Industrial Culture Handbook*. San Francisco: RE/Search Publications, pp. 6, 9, 19, 44.

2 Wilkinson CJ. 2008. John Lennon's 'Revolution 9.' *Perspectives of New Music* 46(2): 226–7.

3 Stapleton S, Fothergill J, Pathak H. 1979. [Nurse with Wound List]. Liner notes to: *Chance Meeting on a Dissecting Table of a Sewing Machine and an Umbrella*. Hastings: United Dairies.

4 Harley J. 2002. CD Program Notes. *Computer Music Journal* 26(4): 122.

5 Reed SA. 2013. *Assimilate: A Critical History of Industrial Music.* Oxford: Oxford University Press, p. 43.

6 Toniutti G. 2022. Personal communication.

7 Vale V, Juno A. 1983, p. 131.

8 ibid., p. 133.

9 Humon N. 2021. Personal communication.

10 Xenakis I. 2002. *Persepolis + Remixes Edition I* CD [ASPHODEL LTD 2005]. San Francisco: Asphodel.

11 Harley J. 2005. The Creative Compositional Legacy of Iannis Xenakis. In: *Definitive Proceedings of the 'International Symposium Iannis Xenakis' (Athens, May 2005)*. Ed. by Georgaki A, et al. Athens: National and Kapodistrian University of Athens, pp. 331–7.

12 Xenakis I. 2000. *Persepolis* CD [FractalOX]. Neuilly-sur-Seine: Fractal Records.

13 Xenakis I. 2003. *Iannis Xenakis* CD [Ed. RZ 1015–16]. Berlin: Edition RZ.

14 Xenakis I. 1972. *Persepolis* LP [Philips 6521 045]. Paris: Philips. This edition was reissued in Japan (Philips SFX-8683) in 1974 with very different cover art (non-Heliophore). There were five more reissues all using the original Philips catalog number, each identifiable by slight variations in center label text and price code, and each with a Heliophore cover design.

15 Friedl R. 2009. Polyphone Monophonie: Interpretation und Freiheit in Iannis Xenakis' elektroakustischer Musik. *MusikTexte* 122.

16 Herbst T. 2021. Personal communication.

17 Friedl R. 2022. Personal communication.

18 Xenakis I. 2021. *Electroacoustic Works* LP boxset [KR092]. Berlin: Karlrecords

19 Sivansan S. 2019. Persepolis Now? https://mapmagazine. co.uk/persopolis-now

20 Andrégui P. 1971.

21 Sivansan S. 2019.

22 Teige D. 2022. Personal communication. Due to a communication breakdown with the laser company Teige had retained, real lasers weren't deployed. Also, a helicopter was considered, just as Xenakis had wanted for the original polytope, but this was too expensive. As it turned out, an LAPD helicopter happened to be overhead for part of the evening.

23 Swed M. 2010. Cold, Stern and So Very Hip. Esoteric Composer Iannis Xenakis Is Getting Rock Star Treatment Nine Years after His Death. *Los Angeles Times*, November 10, p. D4.

24 Cantwell N. 2021. Personal communication.

Photographic Credits

p. 16.   Iannis Xenakis in Athens, c.1938. © Iannis Xenakis Family DR. Courtesy of Iannis Xenakis Archives.

p. 19.   A wartime demonstration in Athens, 1930s. Xenakis is second from left. © Athens War Museum. Courtesy of Iannis Xenakis Archives.

p. 27.   *Metastaseis* 'score' (1954). © Iannis Xenakis Family DR. Courtesy of Iannis Xenakis Archives [om-1-4].

p. 40.   The Philips Pavilion, 1958 World's Fair, Brussels. Courtesy of Wouter Hagens.

p. 46.   The Cyrus Cylinder, British Museum. © Marie-Lan Nguyen.

p. 61.   Persepolis, Palace of Darius. Courtesy of Diego Delso, delso. photo, License CC-BY-SA.

p. 66.   *Persepolis* 'score.' © Iannis Xenakis Family DR. Courtesy of Iannis Xenakis Archives [om-27-4-3-p003].

p. 76.   Map of the Persepolis ruin. © Donald Wilbur.

p. 78.   Iannis Xenakis at the control board, Persepolis, August 1971. Photographic © Malie Letrange. © Iannis Xenakis Family DR. Courtesy of Iannis Xenakis Archives.

p. 79.   Torch-bearing schoolchildren from Shiraz spell out *We Bear the Light of the Earth* in Persian during the Persepolis Polytope, August 26, 1971. A still from Pierre Andrégui's 1971 film, *Xenakis: Persepolis*.

p. 96.   A page from *Ettela'at*, January 7, 1978.

p. 106. Technicians control the sound experience at the Polytope de Persépolis reenactment, Los Angeles, November 6, 2010. © Nancy Cantwell.

Index

Abbas the Great 56
Acropolis 20
Alam, Asadollah 90
Alexander the Great 48, 54, 64,
    87, 89, 96
Anargyrion & Korgialenios
    School of Spetses 14
Anastenaria (composition) 26, 37
Andrégui, Pierre 75, 105, 128 n.3
Artaxerxes I 77
Arts-relais 34
Aryanism 49–50
Athens 10–11, 13, 15, 17, 21
Athens Polytechnic 15, 25
Attali, Jacques 7

Bayle, François 37, 68
Beecham, Sir Thomas 32
Beethoven, Ludwig van 14
Berlin 104–5
Bohor (composition) 99, 101
Boulez, Pierre 37
Boushehri, Mehdi 59
Brǎila (Romania) 13
Bread and Puppet Theater 58
British Museum 45–6
Brooks, Peter 90

Cage, John 58
Cantwell, Nancy 106–7
Chandigarh 39–40
Churchill, Winston 18

CineChamber 102–3
Cinema Rex 95
Club d'Essai 8, 34–5, 38, 68
Concret PH (composition)
    38–42, 98, 116 n.36
Constantine II of Greece 82
Corbusier, Le 24–6, 28, 39–43
Couvent de la Tourette. *See*
    Sainte Marie de la Tourette
Crete 14
Crosby, Bing 33
Cunningham, Merce 57–8, 93
Cyrus Cylinder 45–8, 118 n.5,
    119 n.8
Cyrus the Great 45–8, 50, 53–4,
    80, 82, 85, 118 n.5, 119 n.7

Darius the Great 54, 61, 65, 77
Dekemvriana (December
    events) 13, 19–20
Déserts (composition) 9, 36
Diamorphoses (composition) 7,
    38–9, 75, 107
Dodecanese 22, 24
Donaueschinger Musiktage 9,
    29, 37
Dvořák, Antonín 32

EAM. *See* National Liberation
    Front
École Normale de Musique de
    Paris 35

Eimert, Herbert 36
Einstein, Albert 10
ELAS. *See* Greek People's
    Liberation Front
Elektronische Musik 36, 104
Entartete Kunst (Degenerate Art)
    (exhibit) 6–7
Entartete Musik (Degenerate
    Music) (exhibit) 7
EPON. *See* United Panhellenic
    Organization of Youth
État français 23
Ettela'at (newspaper) 96
Expo 58. *See* 1958 Brussels
    World's Fair

Fallaci, Oriana 49
Ferdowsi 50
Ferrari, Luc 37–8, 67
Fibonacci Set 11, 27–8
Fleuret, Maurice 88
Fowles, John 14
France 23, 60, 103
Friedl, Reinhold 103–5
Futurism 1, 5–6

Ghaffari, Farrokh 58, 92
Gharbzadegi (Occidentosis)
    (concept and book) 80, 94
Ghotbi, Reza 56–7, 92
Ghotbi, Sharazad 57
Goléa, Antoine 29
Greece xii, xiii, 14–22, 24, 60, 72
Greek Civil War 21
Greek People's Liberation Front
    (ELAS) 18–19, 21
Greek Resistance 11, 13, 17–22,
    71, 91

Gregory, André 75
Große Deutsche
    Kunstausstellung, Die (Great
    German Art Exhibition)
    (exhibit) 6
Grotowski, Jerzy 59
Groupe de Recherches
    Musicales (GRM) 36–8, 41
Groupe de Recherche de
    Musique Concrète (GRMC).
    See Groupe de Recherches
    Musicales

Hafez 57, 59
Hardelin, Jacques 70
Héliophore technique 70, 135
    n.14
Henry, Pierre 35, 37–8, 68, 99,
    114 n.10
Herbst, Thomas 104
Herodotus 54
Hitler, Adolf 6–7, 18, 33
Honegger, Arthur 23, 25
Hugo, Victor 14
Humon, Naut 102–3
Hyperbolic paraboloid 41
Hyperprism (composition) 3, 7

Industrial Music 5, 99–100
Intolleranza (composition) 3
Iran xii, 11–13, 47, 50–7, 67, 72,
    77, 80, 87, 94, 96, 106
Iranian Revolution xii, 72, 93,
    97–8
Isfahan 56, 121 n.3

Kandinsky, Vasiliy 5
Kapuściński, Ryszard 97

Karkowski, Zbigniew 103
Kayhan International
(newspaper) 87, 89
Khomeini, Ruhollah xii, 48,
89–90, 94–7
Kissinger, Henry xii
Klaw Theater (New York) 3
Koundouroff, Aristotelis 15

La Légende d'Eer (composition)
99, 105
Le Monde (newspaper) 60, 90, 99
Leroy, Maurice 47
Ligeti, György 36
'Lord Byron' brigade 18
Los Angeles 106–7

Mâche, François-Bernard 37
Magnetic tape 23, 32
Magnetophone 32–3
Mahlouji, Vali 105
Manichaeism 71–2, 81, 90
Mashayekhi, Alireza 81
Marx, Karl 17, 94
Marathon (town) 15
Maxim's de Paris 84
Merzbow 99, 103
Messiaen, Olivier 25–6, 35–8
Metastaseis (composition) 9–11,
26–9, 62, 113 n.14
Metaxas, Ioannis 15
Milhaud, Darius 23, 25
Minu-Sepehr, Aria 52
Mission for My Country (book)
51, 55
Modulor 28
Mozart, Wolfgang Amadeus
15, 32

Mullin, Maj. Jack 33
Mumma, Gordon 58, 93
Musica Futurista (composition)
1–3
Musique concrète 11, 34– /, 66,
68, 75

Najaf 95
Naqsh-e Rostam 65, 77–9, 83, 87
National Liberation Front (EAM)
18–19, 21
National Socialism 6–8, 10–11,
15–18, 20, 23, 32, 91
Nazis. *See* National Socialism
1958 Brussels World's Fair
39–40, 42
Noël Paton, Esmeade 14
Nono, Luigi 3
Nuits (composition) 59–62, 90

Orient-Occident (composition)
100

Pahlavi, Empress Farah 52,
56–8, 82, 85–6, 88–9, 95,
131 n.50
Pahlavi, Mohammad Reza Shah
xii, 12, 46, 48–56, 58, 60, 63,
80, 82–4, 86, 89, 92–8, 118
n.5
Pahlavi, Princess Ashraf 46
Pahlavi, Reza Shah 50–1
Paris 23–5, 40, 52, 56, 99
Parmegiani, Bernard 37, 99
Parsons, Anthony 93–4
Pasargadae 45–6, 54, 82
Persephassa (composition) 61,
65, 124 n.24

Persepolis (composition and album) xii, xiii, 1, 7, 11–12, 48, 60, 65–70, 77, 89–90, 92, 99–107

Persepolis (site) 45, 47, 50, 57, 61, 64–5, 68–9, 75, 78–9, 82–3, 85–9, 96

Persia 45–50, 53–4, 63, 65, 81

Persian Empire. *See* Persia

Pfleumer, Fritz 32

Philippot, Michel 37–8

Philips Pavilion 10, 39–43, 62, 117 n.38

Philips (record label) 68, 70, 99, 103, 135 n.14

Philips Studios (Eindhoven) 40, 42, 119 n.7

Pig, Child, Fire (play) 93, 95

Pindar 14

Plato 15, 17, 54

Poème électronique (composition) 39–42, 62

Polytope de Montréal 62–3

Polytope de Persépolis 43, 62, 65, 68, 72, 75, 86–7, 105

Pratella, Francesco Balilla 1, 5, 7, 10

Prometheus 72

Qom 97

Radio Luxembourg 33

Radiodiffusion-Télévision Française (RTF) 34

Ranger, Richard 33

Restagno, Enzo 59

Rezvani, Serge 90

Rhythm & Noise 99, 102

Rimsky-Korsakov, Nikolai 32

Royan Festival 59, 90

Russolo, Luigi 3–5, 7–8

Saadi 57

Sacre du printemps, Le (ballet) 2–3, 7, 9

Sainte Marie de la Tourette 26, 28, 43

Samuel, Claude 59

Sappho 14

SAVAK 56, 60, 81

Schaeffer, Pierre 7, 33–8, 68, 114 n.10

Schönberg, Arnold 7

Serialism 7, 29–30, 37

Shawcross, William 95

Shiraz 45, 57–8, 68, 72, 75, 77, 79, 82, 88, 90, 92–5

Shiraz Festivals xii, 48, 56–9, 61, 63–5, 75, 80–1, 85, 90, 92–4, 98, 105, 119 n.7

Squat Theater 93

Stochastic music 13

Stockhausen, Karlheinz 36–7, 58, 67, 80–1, 89, 94, 99–100, 104, 110 n.1

Stravinsky, Igor 2–3, 7, 9

Strobel, Heinrich 29

Studio Acousti (Paris) 68

Studio d'Essai. *See* Club d'Essai

Studio für elektronische Musik des Westdeutschen Rundfunks (Cologne) 36

Studios Philips (Paris) 41

Taheri, Amir 87–8

Teatro Costanzi (Rome) 1, 3

Tehran 51–2, 56–7, 68, 87, 95, 99
Tehran Journal (newspaper) 88
Teige, Daniel 104–6
Terretektorh (composition) 59
Théâtre des Champs-Élysées
    (Paris) 2, 9
Tjeknavorian, Loris 85, 131 n.49
Toniutti, Giancarlo 100–2
12-tone technique. *See*
    Serialism
2500th Anniversary of the
    Founding of the Persian
    Empire xii, 46–8, 53, 63–5,
    81–6, 89–90, 95, 98, 119 n.7

Underwood, James 88
Unité d'Habitation 24
United Panhellenic
    Organization of Youth
    (EPON) 18

Vafeiadis, Markos 21
Varèse, Edgard 3, 7, 9, 25, 36,
    39–40, 42
Ville cosmique 62

Wilson, Robert 58

Xenakis, Françoise 25, 79
Xenakis, Iannis xii, xiii, 1, 7, 9–11,
    13–30, 37–43, 48, 58–73,
    75–81, 85–92, 95–6, 99–105
Xenakis, Klearchos 14, 22
Xenakis, Photini 14
Xenophon 54
Xerxes the Great 54, 75–6

Zahedi, Ardeshir 84
Zoroastrianism 45, 70–2, 81, 85,
    89, 90, 126 n.15
Zyia Kathisto (Composition) 26

Index